DESCARTES'S LEGACY:
MINDS AND MEANING IN EARLY MODERN PHILOSOPHY

Debates current in the philosophy of mind regarding the gathering and processing of information, and the nature of perception and representation, also animated some of the most important figures in early modern philosophy, among them Descartes, Hume, and Berkeley. The authors of *Descartes's Legacy: Minds and Meaning in Early Modern Philosophy* use certain problems in contemporary information theory to elucidate the concerns of the early modern philosophers. This critical study attempts to uncover what was once called the logic of the theory of ideas, and to explore the questions it was meant to solve, given the limits of the ontological categories available.

The authors begin their discussion of Descartes by examining his response to established models of perception in light of his understanding of the contemporary new science. Since Descartes proposed that any likeness between representation and the thing represented was unreliable, what was his solution to how an internal representation, an idea, gives us information? The authors' central claim is that Descartes's answer to the problem of how the mind knows matter involves a theory of 'intentional ideas.' This provocative divergence from recent discussions of Descartes's philosophy of mind, which have revolved around whether he is a 'realist' or a 'representationalist,' leads the authors to consider the idealism of Hume and Berkeley in light of Descartes's notion of the intentional. Hume and Berkeley, they maintain, explored alternatives to Descartes's conception, which led them to abandon traditional notions of meaning and truth. *Descartes's Legacy* concludes by suggesting that Descartes's picture can be reconciled with twentieth-century materialism, and asking whether the philosophy of mind can live without a primitive notion of the intentional.

By shedding light on Descartes's crucial ontological innovation and on Hume's and Berkeley's reactions to it, the authors of *Descartes's Legacy* have repositioned early modern philosophy within a truly contemporary framework.

DAVID HAUSMAN and ALAN HAUSMAN are members of the Philosophy Department at Southern Methodist University. They have published many articles related to the subject of this book in the *Canadian Journal of Philosophy* and the *History of Philosophy Quarterly* among other journals.

DAVID B. HAUSMAN and ALAN HAUSMAN

Descartes's Legacy:
Minds and Meaning in
Early Modern Philosophy

UNIVERSITY OF TORONTO PRESS
Toronto Buffalo London

© University of Toronto Press Incorporated 1997
Toronto Buffalo London
Printed in Canada

ISBN 0-8020-0947-6 (cloth)
ISBN 0-8020-7957-1 (paper)

B
822
.H38
1997

Printed on acid-free paper

Toronto Studies in Philosophy
Editors: James R. Brown and Calvin Normore

Canadian Cataloguing in Publication Data

Hausman, David B.
  Descartes's legacy : minds and meaning in early modern
  philosophy

  (Toronto studies in philosophy)
  Includes bibliographical references and index.
  ISBN 0-8020-0947-6 (bound)   ISBN 0-8020-7957-1 (pbk.)

  1. Descartes, René, 1596–1650.   2. Berkeley, George,
  1685–1753.   3. Hume, David, 1711–1776.   4. Idea (Philosophy)
  – History.   5. Philosophy of mind – History.   I. Hausman,
  Alan, 1936–   II. Title.   III. Series.

  B822.H38 1997   121'.4   C96-932326-3

University of Toronto Press acknowledges the financial assistance to its
publishing program of the Canada Council and the Ontario Arts Council.

This book is dedicated to the memory of our parents, Jules and Sara Hausman, in honour of their commitment to education and their devotion to their sons. It is also dedicated to the memory of Nancy Lynn Williams, who, had she lived, would have argued brilliantly with every substantive sentence in this book.

Contents

Acknowledgments

A grant from the College of Humanities of Ohio State University helped us begin the project that became this book. We also received financial assistance and support from Dedman College of Southern Methodist University.

We are grateful for discussions over the years with colleagues and friends: George Pappas, Calvin Normore, Peter King, and Bob Turnbull at Ohio State University; Phil Cummins; Louis Loeb; Edwin B. Allaire; Fred Wilson; Robert Muehlmann; Tom Lennon; Richard Watson; Tony Lisska; Laura Keating; and Martin Rice. Our colleagues at Southern Methodist University patiently listened to us present several portions of this book at departmental colloquia. The Philosophy Department of Denison University made many helpful suggestions after presentations of parts of the manuscript at their colloquia.

For invaluable help on preparing the manuscript we wish to thank Ms Diana Grumbles, Ms Kathee Rebernak, Ms Deborah Reynolds, and Ms Diane McFadin. Ms Susan Randall showed remarkable patience and support during the long hours which her husband, David Hausman, spent away from his family.

Writing a book with a co-author can be a rewarding experience; with one's brother, it is a wonderful experience. If any reader enjoys reading this work even a fraction as much as we enjoyed writing it together, we shall feel even happier.

Introduction

This book presents a structural analysis of the seventeenth and early eighteenth centuries' theory of ideas by relating historical philosophy of mind to recent philosophy of mind. Our primary goal here is to uncover what was once aptly called the *logic* of the theory of ideas – the problems it was meant to solve, given the parameters of the ontological categories available.

Such an analysis is necessarily selective in two ways. First, our aim is not to interpret the entire work of any particular philosopher, either to render that work consistent or to show its large lines of development. Take, for example, our treatment of Descartes. Like Russell after him, Descartes wrote a great deal about central metaphysical topics, and sometimes, Descartes changed his mind about things. One example, which we will develop in this book, is the theory of innate ideas. Sometimes, Descartes speaks of an innate idea as if it is merely the potential for acquiring a certain mental content, a view with which even Locke might agree.[1] At other times, he has a much richer view of the content of innate ideas. In the *Meditations*, it is clear that he does not consider all ideas to be innate. In 'Comments on a Certain Broadsheet,' Descartes greatly extends the range of innate ideas – even colour ideas are alleged to be innate.[2] Here, we are concerned with the theory of ideas as a logical thread that links together Descartes's solutions and his epistemological worries: worries about knowledge of the world outside of him. We therefore select for examination only some of what he says about innate ideas, and the reason he changed his mind on this issue is particularly relevant to our story. To put the point slightly differently, we are interested in an analysis, not of Descartes *per se*, but of a set of ideas he promulgated.

Second, ours is not a postmodern approach to history. While we deal extensively with Descartes's central metaphysical view, we make no pretense that we fit either the historical theory of ideas or its contemporary image into the richness of detail of the entire systems of the early modern philosophers, let alone of such current figures as Fodor and Dennett. We take the admittedly controversial position that, to a certain extent, problems can be separated from their immediate cultural context because of their universality. We believe that such themes are independent of context and are the ontological underpinnings of the rich details of cultural history. This is not to deny that we might have written a different book that dealt with less major figures in the seventeenth century who certainly had important things to say about the theory of ideas, such as Foucher, Desgabets, and Toland, as well as major figures such as Malebranche and Leibniz. Our selectivity is again guided by what we believe to be a central logical theme concerning ideas, and in writing about Descartes, Berkeley, and Hume, we believe we have sounded many of its major chords.[3]

An analogy that we hope elucidates our point is the development of transportation from ancient times to the present. We had the horse, then the wheel and the wagon, then the train, and then the automobile and airplane. Each piece of technology was, of course, a product of the limits and genius of the cultural and economic *milieu*. But everyone from the Egyptians to da Vinci to Henry Ford and the Wright brothers was guided by a central logic that transcended the *milieu* – how to get from point A to point B in the most efficient way. Whatever the device, it must be able to stop and go, to carry passengers, to carry them safely, and so on. Naturally, if one looks at da Vinci's drawings of transportation machines, one sees the beauty of the conception within the limits of the sixteenth century. Divesting da Vinci's drawings of their detail and merely seeing them as transportation machines may strike one as destroying the aesthetics of that conception; that isn't, one might say, the real da Vinci. But one cannot and must not deny that he was drawing transportation machines, or else, in the beauty of detail, one misses the point of the enterprise. We do not present the whole historical Descartes; what we hope to do is present the point of his enterprise – to set out the details of the logic of the problems that must be solved if we are to have knowledge of the world beyond our own ideas.

It is for this reason that we believe that certain *current* problems in information theory can be used to elucidate early modern philosophy, and vice versa. Information-theoretic questions, especially as formulated by early functionalist philosophers, have a clarity and precision that, in our opinion, many isomorphic discussions in history of philosophy have heretofore lacked. If some see, in importing such current terminology, merely a rehash of what has gone on long before, we think it is because the new vocabulary has so swiftly insinuated itself into current thinking. What has not been provided, and what we hope this book does provide, is an essential linkage between the old and the new.

In selecting Descartes, Berkeley, and Hume for examination, we have chosen what might justifiably be considered the most extreme solutions to the problems engaged by early functionalism. Yet these extremes are compelling precisely because they present alternatives that seem difficult to avoid. Extremes, after all, are parameters, limits. Contemporary philosophers of mind, in attempting to answer questions of how information about the world is internalized and processed, have not clearly seen these alternatives in the early moderns, and have subsequently failed to see the full logic of their own positions.[4]

In addition to presenting the theory of ideas, there is a second motivation for this book. We are dismayed by the number of contemporary philosophers working on current problems who ignore the relevance of the history of philosophy to their solutions. One source of current philosophical practice is the hegemony of science over modern intellectual life, which, of course, includes philosophical life. Many scientists believe that the history of their area is irrelevant to their own work: since progress is made, the history of science is seen as the history of mistakes. Many philosophers agree that science and philosophy are not essentially different. We believe, rather, that the role of history is one of the key differences between philosophy and science. Philosophy consists of a small set of interrelated problems. The use of the history of philosophy is essential if progress is to be made.

This book has a hero – Descartes – the first great philosophical innovator of the modern era. Far from treating Descartes simply as the last significant medieval philosopher, we see him responding in a new way to certain key philosophical problems. The new science requires a fresh response to issues concerning perception, and that Descartes believes this is so is clearly stated in the *Optics*.[5] He wants to know how we get information from and about the external world, given the new theories of science. More specifically, the issue concerns how an internal representation – an idea – gives us information. Likeness between representation and represented is not going to hold up, given the nature of the causal interaction between the perceiver and the world. What Descartes puts in place of a likeness principle – what we call 'intentional ideas' – marks what he and some modern figures saw as his crucial ontological innovation.

In contrast to Descartes's theory of intentional ideas, we develop an explication of the idealism of Berkeley and Hume. In an important respect, they represent a throwback to the medievals, because neither understands how a representation could be anything but like what it represents. Yet, because they cannot incorporate likeness between the carrier and the object of information within their new causal theories, they bring the object of perception itself into the mind. Unable to comprehend how we get information from the external world, they are forced to the extreme of abandoning traditional notions of meaning and truth.

This book is not a defence of an intentional theory of mind. It is, however, a reminder of the problems such a theory is meant to solve. Many modern materialists believe that traditional intentional theories are incompatible with their views and that no adequate theory of mind can take the notion of the intentional as incapable of analysis. Things are not quite so simple. Searle, for example, in *The Rediscovery of the Mind*, forcefully points out that the intentional is not incompatible with materialism. We are not suggesting that current cognitive theory is unaware of the existence of the Cartesian theory of ideas; we do think, however, that the logic of the Cartesian position considers the modern view as an option. In addition, we hope to have shown that, although Descartes, in a sense, does take intentionality of ideas as primitive, there is a great deal one can say to elucidate the concept. For example, there is a perfectly good sense in which a Cartesian theory of ideas can live with scientific behaviourism. The real question in philosophy of mind is whether we can live *without* a primitive notion of the intentional. This, of course, remains to be seen. Our effort will have been successful if the historical discussion in this book helps others see what needs to be seen.

DESCARTES'S LEGACY:
MINDS AND MEANING IN EARLY MODERN
PHILOSOPHY

1

Machines, Meaning, and the Theory of Ideas

If you like, think of the machine quite crudely, as a box on wheels which, at any stage of the computation, is over some square of the tape. The tape is like a rail-road track; the ties mark the boundaries of the squares; and the machine is like a very short car, capable of moving along the track in either direction ... At the bottom of the car there is a device that can read what's written between the ties; erase such stuff; and write symbols there.

The machine is designed in such a way that at each stage of the computation it is in one of a finite number of internal *states*, q_1, ... , q_m. Perhaps the simplest way to picture the thing is ... : Inside the box there is a man, who does all the reading and writing and erasing and moving.[1]

In this simple description of the operations of a Turing machine, there lies a profound set of philosophical problems. The machine consists of a segmented tape with symbols written on each segment. The machine *scans* the segments for *information* and then, on the basis of that information, makes a computation. The example suggests alternative ways of describing how an information-processing entity receives input from a source outside itself and processes it; the processor is an intelligence or, alternatively, a machine (or, perhaps more accurately, to paraphrase Boolos and Jeffrey's point, the machine can be described as an intelligence). Those alternatives, if both do indeed accurately describe the process, need reconciliation; at least, it is not clear that they are compatible. Modern philosophy of mind, notably functionalism, dedicates itself to exploring this tension. But, despite what functionalists may believe, the problem is not new. The same tension was present in the seventeenth and early eighteenth centuries: the theory of ideas was a direct response to it. Showing this is the task of this book.

Much has been written about the seventeenth-century theory of ideas and its ultimate demise. For example, everyone knows the easy criticism – which was also believed to be the fatal one – that the Cartesian theory of ideas leads to instant failure: if ideas represent, how do we know what they represent unless we are somehow already aware of the entities represented (such knowledge being precluded by the very theory in question)? But putting this criticism together with other aspects of the theory of ideas – for example, the primary–secondary quality distinction, the place of direct awareness in apprehending ideas, the function of innate ideas, the causation of ideas, the role of God as guarantor of truth – is hardly an easy task. In this book, we want to organize these issues around what we think are basic models for the problems faced by idea theorists of the early modern period. These models are provided by the dual descriptions of the information processor discussed in the previous paragraph. We do not think that foisting the structure of the Turing-machine situation – data, scanner, instructions, action – onto the seventeenth century anachronistic; in fact, we shall argue that it is not. Central to the two models, the interpretations of this structure, is not just the place of the mind in nature, but the nature of the mind itself.

The issue of an exact characterization of the mental in Cartesian and post-Cartesian thought, we believe, has not been adequately addressed.[2] The Turing-machine example focuses attention on the characterization of the mental in the seventeenth century, just as it does in today's philosophy of mind. Indeed, we believe it can be plausibly argued that the notion of mental *content* has been the *bête noire* of recent philosophy of mind; given the current obsession with some variety of materialism, no one can figure out how to accommodate it.[3] But we believe that this was also a problem for the seventeenth century; the new science created the spectre of materialism and what, in effect, was a functionalist theory of mind. The reaction to this spectre was the theory of ideas.

By using the phrase 'spectre of materialism,' we do not mean to imply that Descartes was, all along, an implicit dualist who felt that materialism must be purged to save the mind for, say, theological reasons. Rather, we shall argue that Descartes was forced to dualism because he believed states of bodies are incapable of having the semantic properties necessary to an adequate theory of perception. Physical objects and events cannot serve as information carriers. Such carriers must have a very special set of properties. This is a new notion of semantics, we believe, and it sharply separates him from the medievals. Today, of course, there are so-called causal theories of semantics which allow brain states to have what these theorists claim are the analogue of semantic properties. We shall show why Descartes did not espouse such an alternative, though he clearly saw its possibilities and clearly appreciated the central importance of different views of causation for semantics. It is, we shall argue, Descartes's theory of ideas which then sets the tone for the debate about the properties of ideas in the seventeenth and early eighteenth centuries.

To some philosophers, problems with the theory of ideas are intimately tied to the classic categories of mind and body. In their early work, Fodor and Dennett took what they believed to be a fresh look at these categories, which they understand in terms of Cartesian dualism.[4] Not only do the categories lead to insoluble problems – for example, causal interaction – but, even ignoring these problems, they fail to do justice to our knowledge about what in ordinary life we take to be mental and physical states. Fodor and Dennett see, behind the traditional categories, an attempt to solve the problems identified in the first paragraph of this chapter. The central issue is the acquisition of information from the physical world by an intelligent being. As Dennett sees it, the theory of ideas of the seventeenth century is invoked to explain how an intelligence gets information from an internal representation, or an idea. In both his view and Fodor's, all who subscribed to this tradition, whether or not they acknowledged it, invoked an *homunculus*, an intelligence, to explain how information was derived from internal representations.

Early functionalists devote a good deal of attention to problems with homunculi. Even so, it remains unclear whether they recognize the extent to which the notion of the homunculus is linked to that of a concept that we shall argue is also crucial to seventeenth-century philosophy of mind, the *intentional*.[5] By 'the intentional' we mean the content of mental states. Sometimes the notion of the intentional is taken in a more commonsensical way, merely to indicate beliefs, desires, and so on – the propositional attitudes, what we ordinarily take to be the referents of the intentional verbs – and their connections. These connections between mental states are provided by what has come to be called 'folk psychology,' the loose system of teleologically based explanations we use in everyday life to interpret and predict human behaviour.[6] Fodor's and Dennett's analysis of folk psychology, as they understand the tradition before them, is conducted in terms of the homunculus. In the remainder of this chapter, we wish to explore the reasons why functionalists are dissatisfied with homunculi. Their analysis of folk psychology ultimately leads to the first sense of the intentional, the aboutness of internal representations, and therefore to crucial issues about semantics. We shall begin, therefore, with folk psychology.

It is easy to attack folk psychology as an inadequate, low-level science, so arguments against it can provide cheap thrills for those inclined towards reductionism. These arguments hardly provide ammunition against an analysis of what lies at a deeper level, the aboutness of mental states. Early functionalists did try to do justice to folk psychology as the jumping-off point for an adequate philosophy of mind. For them this means at least stating the conditions that a science of psychology must fulfil. Their attack on the homunculus is directed towards what they took to be the *implications* of folk psychology. On their reading, folk-psychological propositions such as 'John perceives a tree' have been, explicitly or implicitly, understood in terms of an intelligence, the homunculus reading an internal representation for tree information.[7] Fodor and Dennett believe that this traditional analysis of internal representations presents an obvious problem: the positing of an intelligence whose capabilities mirror those of the intelligent being with which the analysis began.

As we shall see, the situation is akin to what classical logicians, for example, Russell, did for the notion of a class.[8] Class talk is, to say the least, very useful to mathematicians. Even diehard nominalists like Goodman use it constantly.[9] Doesn't it, then, make perfect sense in its own right? The problems are not in what we shall call the 'common-sense' uses of class talk or, in the case in point, folk psychology. Rather, the problems are with what seems to be implied or assumed by those uses. Russell argued that he knew what the conditions were that classes obeyed but not what a class was – he just couldn't figure out what sort of ontological entity a class could possibly be. Of course, one could answer, a class is that which is identical when its members are, etc., etc., thereby staying within the accepted framework of axioms for class theory. But Russell wanted to know what entities obeyed all these axioms. He finally decided that he could replace class talk with attribute talk, without essential loss. That is, the logical structure of the axioms for class theory also characterized attributes, and he *understood* the nature of attributes.

Fodor and Dennett do something like this with folk psychology. They start with the so-called top-down strategy, with folk psychology as data for analysis. One does not start with inchoate data and expect to get anywhere, and, indeed, both admit that folk psychology provides reasonable explanations for human behaviour. What, then, is wrong with it? Why must we replace it with an analysis which employs none of the terms of folk psychology?

The analogy to Russell invites us to think that there is a sense in which one understands folk psychology and a sense in which one does not. Specifically, Fodor argues against understanding folk psychology in terms of the homunculus. More specifically, the argument is against the interpretation or model of information processing that invokes an homunculus as the processor. Put into the Russellian analogy, invoking an homunculus is similar to repeating the axioms for classes in an attempt to clarify the notion of class. One avoids such triviality in the same way that Russell did, by finding a set of entities we do understand and which have, in a sense yet to be specified clearly, the same structural properties as those we don't understand. Attributes have the same logical properties as classes. Turing machines, if early functionalist theory is correct, mirror the logical properties of the facts of folk psychology. But, rather obviously, claiming that invocation of the homunculus repeats the mysteries of folk psychology is pejorative only if one sees the latter as mysterious. There are those, after all, who see *attributes* as mysterious, and there are those who think there is nothing at all mysterious about grasping the meaning of an internal representation. So, once again, what are the mysteries that Fodor and Dennett see?

Some philosophers are suspicious of functionalism because it seems too easy. Since functionalism licenses the individuation of states by reference to their causal role, it appears to allow a trivial explanation of any observed event E, that is, it appears to postulate an E-causer. For example, what makes the valves in a machine open? Why, the operation of a valve opener. And what is a valve opener? Why, anything that has the functionally defined property of causing valves to open.

In psychology this kind of question-begging often takes the form of theories that in effect postulate *homunculi* with the selfsame intellectual capacities the theorist set out to explain. Such is the case when visual perception is explained by simply postulating psychological mechanisms that process visual information. The behaviorist has often charged the mentalist, sometimes justifiably, of mongering this kind of question-begging pseudo explanation. The charge will have to be met if functionally defined mental states are to have a serious role in psychological theories.

The burden of the accusation is not untruth but triviality. There can be no doubt that it is a valve opener that opens valves, and it is likely that visual perception is

mediated by the processing of visual information. The charge is that such puta-
tive functional explanations are mere platitudes. The functionalist can meet this
objection by allowing functionally defined theoretical constructs only where
mechanisms exist that can carry out the function and only where he has some
notion of what such mechanisms might be like. One way of imposing this requirement is to identify the mental processes that psychology postulates with the operations of the restricted class of possible computers called Turing machines.[10]

Let's try to get at Fodor's meaning by using an example. A particular
human behaviour – let us say, seeing a tiger and running away from it –
can be thought of as involving input and output. Suppose we explain
the output as follows: there is a visual information processor which,
upon processing the tiger information, makes the decision to run from
the tiger. But what is the nature of this processor? One could claim that
the processor is what is aware of the visual information and makes deci-
sions on its basis. Thus the processor is the homunculus. This 'analysis'
of the processor is perceived by Fodor as trivial; indeed, as circular.
Fodor is levelling a charge similar to the triviality charge levelled by
Molière against claiming opium puts one to sleep because it is a sopo-
rific; similar charges were often directed against Aristotelian natures
when seen as mere dispositions. But appeals to natures need not be trivial *per se*. One can look at such appeals as promissory notes. There must
be something that explains how the input produces the output, and the
dispositional term is like a variable whose value is to be determined.
Filling the variable with the proper sort of functions is obligatory.

What are the proper sorts of functions? A class of pairs of inputs and
outputs is thought of as a function. Fodor claims that the functionalist
will fill in the promissory note represented by the invocation of an information processor, the entity that transforms input into output, with
realizable devices. The folk psychologist will provide a teleological
account: she ran from the tiger because she desired so-and-so. Indeed, if
the theorist happens to be a Freudian, or a gestalt psychologist, she may
provide a rich set of laws that explain the person's fear of tigers, in addition to a lot of her other behaviour. In what sense is this trivial, not filling in the variable? Are such laws not functional?[11]

Indeed, it seems clear that Fodor cannot object to a Freudian elaboration of folk psychology on such grounds – it certainly is possible that
Freudian or gestalt psychology is a legitimate extension of folk psychology, and that its laws are functional. These laws, of course, are expressed
by using intentional verbs. Intelligent beings remember, desire, love,

believe, and process information. But information processing is not just another human mental activity; it *underlies* all these other activities. So, even if some extension of folk psychology, like Freudian theory, seems to elaborate significantly the notion of an information processor, we are, in fact, still left with information processing to explain. Notice, however, that there is nothing whatever trivial in the elaboration of folk psychology provided by Freudian and gestalt theory. Indeed, they may well provide models of explanation for human behaviour and would thus have to be incorporated into the data of any top-down strategy. Rather, Fodor is pointing to something that these theories, and folk psychology itself, take for granted – the processing of information (much like mathematicians took addition for granted before Cantor, Peano, and Russell). Such processing seems to underlie every cognitive act, and perhaps even affective states. Trying to determine the nature of information processing is thus foundational, and, as in all foundational questions, one is treading on what used to be considered a border between science and philosophy. Even if we reject this distinction, as so many today do, we must be very careful about what questions we are raising, let alone the answers we give.

There is, first of all, a scientific question (or a series of scientific questions) about the possibility of a scientific psychology. The early functionalists argue that such a possibility is realizable only in a mechanistic system, and that homunculus theory precludes such mechanization (unless the invocation of a homunculus is just a shorthand way of making a promise that a mechanism will be provided once we know more than we currently do). We wish to illustrate in this book how the existence of a full-blown homunculus is compatible with the existence of a scientific psychology in the Fodor–Dennett sense. Our point is that a scientific psychology is not concerned with problems of meaning; Descartes, as we show in chapter 2, adopts a theory of meaning which is homuncular in so far as he treats the intentional as irreducible. Descartes's theory of ideas, as we shall demonstrate, is a response to a sceptical problem which derives from Descartes's worries about semantics. But considerations of systematic scepticism play no role in scientific psychologies. What this illustrates is that the function of the homunculus need not be causal – that is, there are no laws of psychology which need to include homunculi as values of their variables. Rather, we shall show, an homunculist theorist may claim that homunculi are needed to solve certain sorts of semantic problems. Thus, one cannot dismiss the homunculus easily on grounds of triviality.

To provide variations on the position reflected in the previous paragraph is, in effect, one of the major tasks of this book. What we wish to do now is to give a sketch of some of the steps that we hope to fill in, in later chapters. We are not maintaining that anyone in the seventeenth-century tradition actually constructed an homunculus theory that was compatible with a scientific psychology, though, as we shall see, Descartes comes close. We feel, however, that developing the logic of this position will enable us better to understand both the early modern and twentieth-century views on this issue.

The Turing machine, as we have noted, gives one hope that a science of psychology is, in principle, mechanistically realizable. We have with such a machine a clear idea of its internal representations and how they function causally to produce output behaviour. We can, for example, fully understand the operation of addition without homunculus talk, though such talk, as we have seen, is used for convenience even by mathematicians. We might describe the person in the box as reading information, following instructions, and so on. But to say he is adding 2 and 2 – the model of some cognitive act – is merely to make reference to a series of mechanical moves. The hope is to extend this model to every cognitive process. Now the Turing machine uses internal representations, or ideas. As we usually think of ideas, they are about something. What are the Turing machine's ideas about? What is their content? Functionalists are crystal clear about the answers here: The content of an internal representation is a function of its relationship to other representations, to the instructions which make reference to them, and to the input which produces them and the output which they help produce. That is, the content of a representation is a function of its causal role.

The functionalist view of content is reminiscent of Skinner's. For Skinner, to say a rat is hungry is to say that it is on a certain feeding schedule, and it is time for it to be fed. It is not necessary in such a scheme to refer to an inner state of the rat – namely, the state of being hungry. Whether there are such states, that is, whether rats think of cheese when they are hungry, is, according to Skinner, a question that need not be answered. Suppose that rats do have such inner states. Then, if we can produce a rat psychology, it is because, for Skinner, there is a happy set of laws that provides a correlation between observable rat behaviours and the inner states of rats. Although the functionalist scheme is more complex because it invokes internal representations, one must not be misled into thinking that functionalists are doing what Skinner eschews – namely, appealing to the inner states of rats in some way that takes these inner states as unanalysable, as the homunculist theorist does.[12] If that were what was going on, *the belief that P would be about P independent of the causal relationships in which the belief stands.* By 'independent,' we do not mean that the belief stands in no causal connections. Rather, such beliefs are logically independent of such connections in the sense that the connections are not *constitutive* of content. Not so for the functionalist.

We can best illustrate what is at issue here by considering a case suggested by the 'inverted spectrum' problem. If the case were possible, as it is from the point of view of common-sense folk psychology, the following would occur. First, whenever S has an X-perception, the cause of the perception is Y (where Y is not X), S behaves as if his perception is a Y-perception, and Y behaviour is appropriate to his survival or success. Second, whenever S has a Y-perception, it is caused by X, S behaves as if there is an X, and such behaviour is appropriate. To make the point suggestively, S sees cats and behaves as if they are dogs, and sees dogs and behaves as if they are cats. We can now make the difference between the functionalist and the homunculist theory clear. For the functionalist, if S behaves consistently as if there is an X present, then the internal representation is in fact an X representation and not, as folk psychology claims, a Y one. Looked at from the point of view of the functionalist, then, folk psychology misdescribes the case to begin with. We cannot describe the content of a representation without knowing its causal role.

On the other hand, the homunculist theorist will claim that there is a difference between the case in which S perceives X and exhibits Y behaviour, and the *normal* case in which some subject K perceives Y and exhibits Y behaviour – namely, a difference between the content of the percepts of S and K. It would, under the homunculist view as we have developed it so far, be possible to have a world in which one were systematically mistaken about one's perceptual contents, in the sense that S would believe it was an X-world, when in fact it was a Y-world.

Of course, if one takes the 'inverted spectrum' case as normally stated, one might wish to claim there is a difference between two *qualia* states, for example, seeing red and seeing green, for which functionalism cannot account. For these critics of functionalism, the semantic status of mental states is not necessarily the issue. By extending the case to dog and cat ideas, as we did in the example above, semantics becomes the key issue. Descartes is not willing to allow what happens externally, that is, behaviour, even consistent behaviour, to determine what is true internally in the manner of the functionalists.

There seems, therefore, to be a tension between a Cartesian and functionalist theory of meaning. Which, if either, is compatible with a scientific psychology? As we show in the next two chapters, Descartes at least can embrace both theories, as long as one is concerned only with scientific results – namely, the prediction of human behaviour. Descartes, however, sees his own theory of meaning as a response to a set of philosophical problems which do not impinge on a scientific psychology any more than the problem of illusion impinges on a scientific physics.

But the Cartesian view of semantics seems highly problematic philosophically. Everyone knows that Descartes worries about an evil demon in the *Meditations*. A world in which the counterpart of the inverted spectrum is possible is certainly a world in which *an* evil demon (though, as we show, not the *only* sort of evil demon) is abroad: what could be more insidious than a *systematic* set of false beliefs whose falsehood is in principle undiscoverable? In the next chapter we show that Descartes's semantics clearly illustrate the dimensions of this problem, not because he explicitly considers it, but because other, logically prior, demons determine the sort of answer he can give to the 'inverted spectrum' case.

2

Descartes's Semantic Intentions

... if we bear well in mind the scope of our senses and what it is exactly that reaches our faculty of thinking by way of them, we must admit that in no case are the ideas of things presented to us by the senses just as we form them in our thinking. So much so that there is nothing in our ideas which is not innate to the mind or the faculty of thinking, with the sole exception of those circumstances which relate to experience, such as the fact that we judge that this or that idea which we now have immediately before our mind refers to a certain thing situated outside us. We make such a judgment not because these things transmit the ideas to our mind through the sense organs, but because they transmit something which, at exactly that moment, gives the mind occasion to form these ideas by means of the faculty innate to it. Nothing reaches our mind from external objects through the sense organs except certain corporeal motions ... in accordance with my own principles. But neither the motions themselves nor the figures arising from them are conceived by us exactly as they occur in the sense organs, as I have explained at length in my *Dioptrics*. Hence it follows that the very ideas of the motions themselves and of the figures are innate in us. The ideas of pains, colours, sounds and the like must be all the more innate if, on the occasion of certain corporeal motions, our mind is to be capable of representing them to itself, for there is no similarity between these ideas and the corporeal motions.[1]

In our discussion of Descartes, we take the epistemological issues raised by the *Meditations* to be our (and Descartes's) central philosophical concern. This is not to say, of course, that we restrict our discussion of Descartes to that work, but only that it sets our major themes. Indeed, if one takes Descartes's scientific works such as the *Optics* and *Treatise on Man* as central, one might well come out with a radically different interpretation of his epistemology. Here are the reasons: The scientific works are not primarily epistemological. They do not raise sceptical issues such as the 'evil demon' hypothesis which yield a rich Cartesian semantics; in effect they presuppose that the semantic problems raised by the *Meditations* are resolved. Take, for example, his discussion in the *Optics* of the principle that mental representations must be like what they represent. Descartes rejects this view with a set of highly interesting arguments, but despite some analogies – for example, between the artist's use of line and what those lines represent – he has nothing to put in place of this likeness principle. Thus the *Optics* cries out for a semantical view that Descartes does not provide in it or his other scientific work, and the full ramifications of the rejection of the likeness model are seen only in the *Meditations*. Or take as another example the *Treatise on Man*. Here, Descartes builds a mechanical model of a human being, and the implication is that we can learn much of real humans from the model. But there are no explicitly acknowledged epistemological difficulties here; they are only suggested by the fact that Descartes never provides in this work, and knows he never provides, the relationship between the elaborately constructed model of the brain and corresponding mental states.

Thus, two of his major scientific works clearly lack a view of how the mind knows the world: we believe the *Meditations* fills this gap. Indeed, as we shall show, the *Meditations* view picks up precisely on the crucial semantic *lacunae* in the *Optics*.

The literature on Cartesian semantics has tended to examine the relationship between the physical world and ideas. This is natural enough; mind–body dualism and the problem of interaction make such a move plausible. Unfortunately, *assuming* the mind–body distinction in a discussion of Descartes's semantics also leads one to believe that he faces insoluble semantic problems.[2] We shall argue that, contrary to the force of that assumption, it is his semantics for ideas that *leads* to a new vision of the mind. The mind–body problem is thus a consequence of his view of ideas. However, we shall argue that Descartes does not conceive of escape from the circle of ideas as a direct leap to the physical world. There is a crucial intermediary step that guarantees, without the necessity of invoking God as a non-deceiver, that the existence of at least some of our ideas entails that something exists beyond them. Just as Frege distinguishes the sense of an expression from its reference or, as some would say, meaning from truth, so Descartes distinguishes the question of what our thoughts *mean* from the question of whether there is a physical world. We shall argue that the issues of whether there is such a world and, if there is, what we can know about it can both be resolved by invoking the same secular principles that allow Descartes to break out of the circle of ideas.

In this chapter we present the logical structure of Descartes's position: given that classical theories of perception fail, *ideas can no longer be considered to be like what they are about.* Even analogizing Cartesian ideas to the modern notion of sense data – allegedly unlike the entities that cause them – doesn't help. Thus, Descartes is faced with the problem of showing how representational entities, ideas, can carry out their function without bearing any resemblance to what they represent. There are two ways one can accomplish this: (1) with modern notions of semantics that either (a) have a sentient being assigning a semantics or (b) have a causal or functionalist theory of meaning; and (2) adoption of an intentionalist semantic theory. We argue that the Cartesian texts and the logic of Descartes's position show that (2) is his choice. Here, the theory of innate ideas plays a key role. In this and subsequent chapters we show why Descartes thinks that (1) will not work.

Many philosophers, however, have felt that Descartes's attempts to avoid the semantic pitfalls he himself places in his way end in circularity or absurdity. Arthur Danto is typical of those commentators who feel Descartes ends in semantic disaster. In 'The Representational Character of Ideas and the Problem of the External World,'[3] he presents what in effect is a *reductio* of Descartes's notion of idea. The argument is this: If an idea must be about something, and is true by virtue of the fact that what it is about actually obtains, Descartes must claim that all ideas are true.[4] The reason is that ideas are about their truth conditions, and they could not be ideas and could not be about those truth conditions unless what they were about actually obtained. Danto analogizes ideas to photographs, where we say of the latter that an alleged photo not produced by that of which it is an image is not really a photo. The *reductio* is obvious: the so-called problem of the external world – how can we know from our ideas what facts obtain in the world beyond our ideas – would not be a problem if Descartes's theory of ideas was sound. Yet, Descartes, in labouring under the hypothesis of the evil demon, certainly talks as if ideas must be at least *capable* of falsehood.

Danto claims that ideas are of something, the phrase 'of-x' designating 'a simple property of ideas.'[5] In so far as this merely expresses the intrinsic intentionality of ideas, we can, at least at this point, agree. His conclusion from that characterization is, however, unwarranted. Descartes has a much more complex semantics for ideas than Danto envisions or, perhaps more accurately, actually discusses. Unfortunately, Danto dismisses the very discussion that would have shown him that his analysis fails to do justice to Descartes: 'I shall not pursue here Descartes's fascinating thesis that the causes of ideas must bear some internal relationship to the latters' representational properties – that the idea of a substance must be caused by a substance, even if it be some substance other than the one represented by the idea itself – but merely indicate what I believe to be the causal theory required by him.'[6]

Under our view of Cartesian semantics, the representational character of an idea is a function of the representational properties of its 'parts,' in a way analogous to the standard valuation semantics for a well-formed formula in first-order logic, like 'Fa.'[7] To give a valuation for 'Fa,' one gives a valuation for its terms, and then a characterization of its truth conditions. Thus, even if $V(F)$ picks out, say, a class of entities in a domain, and $V(a)$ some entity or other in that domain, 'Fa' may be false, for example, when $V(a)$ is not a member of $V(F)$. In a standard semantics for first-order logic, of course, there is no question that an assignment can be made to the terms in 'Fa' as a function of the members of some domain. But, for Descartes, one may wonder whether the analogy holds. If John is dreaming of a unicorn, even if we claim that the predicate 'is a unicorn' can be broken down into 'simpler' elements, for example, 'is a horse' and 'has a horn in the middle of its head,' what guarantees that anything exemplifies either property, let alone the two conjunctively? Descartes has answers to these questions. The answers are, as we shall argue, tremendously rich philosophically; they embody an entirely new philosophy of mind.

In the 'painter passage' in the First Meditation, Descartes makes clear that he has a distinction between simple and complex ideas, as suggested by the analogy of the penultimate paragraph:

Suppose then that I am dreaming, and that these particulars – that my eyes are open, that I am moving my head and stretching out my hands – are not true. Perhaps, indeed, I do not even have such hands or such a body at all. Nonetheless, it must surely be admitted that the visions which come in sleep are like paintings, which must have been fashioned in the likeness of things that are real, and hence that at least these general kinds of things – eyes, head, hands and the body as a whole – are things which are not imaginary but are real and exist. For even when painters try to create sirens and satyrs with the most extraordinary bodies, they cannot give them natures which are new in all respects; they simply jumble up the limbs of different animals. Or if perhaps they manage to think up something so new that nothing remotely similar has ever been seen before – something which is therefore completely fictitious and unreal – at least the colours used in the composition must be real. By similar reasoning, although these general kinds of things – eyes, head, hands and so on – could be imaginary, it must at least be admitted that certain other even simpler and more universal things are real. These are as it were the real colours from which we form all the images of things, whether true or false, that occur in our thought.[8]

In effect, Descartes here gives a partial answer to Danto: an idea presents something to us in virtue of the presentation of its constituents. The real issue concerns what is entailed by the presentation of those constituents. Of course, at this point one may invoke, as Descartes himself does, the 'evil demon' hypothesis. Before engaging it, we wish to point out that, even if one can show that hypothesis to be viable, the distinction between simple and complex ideas shows that Danto's claim that every idea as characterized by Descartes must be true is itself false.[9] Indeed, one can only wonder how Danto missed so obvious an alternative; we shall return to what we think a plausible explanation in chapter 4. For now, let us explore what might reasonably be taken to be the core of truth in Danto's paper.

We do maintain, as an essential part of Cartesian semantics, that the existence of every simple idea entails the existence of an entity outside the circle of one's own ideas.[10] In the spirit of Danto, we shall also argue that this guarantee comes from the very nature of simple ideas. Our claim is indeed a strong one, for, if we are correct, this semantic feature of simple ideas, when properly explicated, does not issue from the goodness of God, but from what Descartes considers to be an indubitable principle. To understand the semantics of simple ideas is to see how one defeats the evil demon without God, and thus how one escapes the apparent circularity of the *Meditations*. We believe, in other words, that one can give a completely secular account of Cartesian semantics – which Danto himself suggests – without the pejorative aspects of Danto's analysis.

The key to Cartesian semantics is the distinction between the objective reality of an idea and the formal reality of the cause of that idea. Descartes invokes this distinction in the Third Meditation. Put succinctly, to speak of the objective reality of an idea is to speak of its intrinsic intentionality. We shall develop our evidence for this claim by presenting what we think the logic of an intentionalist position is, seen against the background of Descartes's arguments attacking a semantic principle of likeness of representor to represented.

As a staunch advocate of the new science, Descartes in effect revolutionizes the theory of perception that had been extant since Aristotle. It is his arguments from the new science that place him first in the line of theorists who invoke internal representations, as described in chapter 1. In other words, the description of the Turing machine as an information processor fits Descartes's view of perception. It is these arguments, and not the appeal to some well-known facts of perception (illusion, perspective, error), which motivate Descartes's theory of internal representations. We shall see later where the arguments from perceptual variation fit in Descartes's overall scheme.

There are four distinct reasons why the new science renders the older theory of perception obsolete.[11] First, Descartes makes clear in the *Optics* that sensible species, those entities favoured by the medievals as 'travelling' from the object to the mind, are no longer relevant variables in the new physical explanation of perception:

We must take care not to assume – as our philosophers commonly do – that in order to have sensory perceptions the soul must contemplate certain images transmitted by objects to the brain; or at any rate we must conceive the nature of these images in an entirely different manner from that of the philosophers. For since their conception of the images is confined to the requirement that they should resemble the objects they represent, the philosophers cannot possibly show us how the images can be formed by the objects, or how they can be received by the external sense organs and transmitted by the nerves to the brain.[12]

Descartes's reading of his predecessors is reminiscent of Kuhn's views about the progress of science. The older view served a purpose once, but its concepts are now simply outmoded. Like phlogiston theory later, sensible species were no longer considered characteristics that had explanatory value. *Second*, the view that sensible species 'inform' the mind, and are thus related differently to it than to objects which these forms characterize, is, we think, one to which Descartes is sensitive.[13] As we shall argue, even if one could make sense of the transference of forms from objects to the mind – which, we think, is highly controversial – Descartes's ontology of modes and substances would not accommodate them.[14] *Third*, the scientific object is no longer describable in the same terms as the perceptual object. The perceptual object is described in what we might call 'macro' terms, whereas the relevant variables in scientific laws are not macro properties: properties of the scientific object are now theoretical entities, not directly perceivable. *Fourth*, perceptual objects are describable in terms of both primary and secondary qualities, the scientific object only in terms of primary qualities. Thus the perceptual object and the scientific object are seen to differ radically.[15]

But how different are they? Twentieth-century sense-data theorists, for example, the early Russell and G.E. Moore, espoused a view which is superficially similar to Descartes's. Indeed, many have read sense-data theories into not only Descartes but other philosophers in 'the way of ideas' tradition. On the sense-data view – which we describe in detail below – however, the logic of perceptual facts is the same as that of physical facts; a standard first-order logic will do to describe both.

An ontology with genuine intentional entities cannot be given such a description.[16] A perception that x is F is not characterizable in the same way as the fact that x is F. When we say 'characterizable,' we do *not* mean to suggest a *judgment* made on the basis of the percept, but what can be called (or used to be, before the barrage of recent attacks) a *description* of the *given*; this point, as we shall see much later, Danto misses entirely, and it greatly adds to the confusion which leads to his conclusion. So, 'that x is F' characterizes the perception, but, *within* that perception, F does not characterize x, that is, is not a property of x. Indeed, neither x nor F occurs as a constituent of, say, the visual field. If we can identify the percept with the visual field at a moment, no predication relations obtain within the field. Yet the field presents, as it were, the fact that x is F. The issue of how something can present a fact without itself sharing something, for example, properties, with that fact is of course the mystery of the intentional which has led many to abandon it as a viable answer to semantic questions. The simple–complex distinction that can be made within idea ('Fa') does not entail that the idea itself contains constituents in the sense that the fact it presents contains them. It merely means that, in presenting a fact, it presents the constituents of the fact. It is on the basis of this presentation that judgments about the physical world are ultimately made; but, as we discuss later, these presentations are not themselves judgments.

Let us try to make clearer what we think this notion of intentionality amounts to. One can construe the medieval view as analysing intentionality in terms of a sharing of form by mind and object. A sense-data view, in which a particular exemplifies properties, can also be seen in this way – a sharing of at least structure, if not content, by the representor and the represented. But such views fail to capture the full notion of the intentional as *directional*; after all, any two things, including two physical things, that share properties are not such that each is *about* the other or *presents* the other, even if one causes the other. Of course one can *make* one thing be about another, assign it a pointing feature, as it were; but this is not *intrinsic* intentionality and, as we shall presently show, generates problems in the form of damaging regresses. In pointing to something else, an intentional entity must be more than just another object. An intentional entity, therefore, does not present the fact that a is F by *being* a fact *like* a is F. An intentional entity has a different *structure* than what it presents.

In the *Meditations*, we believe, Descartes makes it clear that his notion of objective reality is equivalent to intentionality of ideas in the sense just described.[17] It is this view of intentionality of ideas that is the heart of Descartes's dualism. A key passage occurs in the Third Meditation. Descartes has just introduced what we shall call the *ex nihilo* principle, that something cannot come from nothing, as a crucial step in his first proof for God's existence. The problem he sets, however, is a general one – the origin of the content of our ideas: 'For just as the objective mode of being belongs to ideas by their very nature, so the formal mode of being belongs to the causes of ideas – or at least the first and most important ones – by *their* very nature. And although one idea perhaps may originate from another, there cannot be an infinite regress here; eventually one must reach a primary idea, the cause of which will be like an archetype which contains formally <and in fact> all the reality <or perfection> which is present only objectively <or representatively> in the idea.'[18]

Notice that the objective mode of being belongs to the idea *by its very nature*. Ideas are not *assigned* a meaning by a sentient being who cognizes them; nor do they *derive* meaning from, say, some set of causal circumstances (these alternatives will be sharpened shortly). Rather, their objective reality, or representational character, is constitutive of what they are: 'insofar as one idea represents one thing and another represents another, they differ widely; and the greater the amount of objective perfection they contain within themselves, the more perfect their cause must be.'[19]

As we have argued, however, this 'perfection' of the cause is not 'transferred' to the effect, or idea: 'For although this cause does not transfer any of its actual or formal reality to my idea, it should not on that account be supposed that it must be less real.'[20]

Suppose one thinks of God for the first time. Given that ideas cannot come from nothing, and that the cause, God, does not transfer formal reality to the effect, where does the content of the idea of God originate? Descartes's answer is that there is an innate idea of God. As we shall argue below, this notion of innate ideas is the key to Descartes's semantics, and to our view that his ideas are intentional. In brief, the point is simply this: holding in the mind an innate idea that had no semantics would amount to having an idea without meaning. But what is the point of an innate idea whose meaning has to be established externally? If ideas are representational by their very nature, and do not derive their content from their cause in the sense of there being a likeness between cause and effect, then what ideas *mean* must be intrinsic to them.[21]

Non-ideas, for example, chairs and stars, do not have such a characteristic. Neither they nor their properties mean anything. Such a radical difference, we believe, leads Descartes to a crucial ontological distinction. Having characterized a new sort of entity, the intentional internal representation, and still immersed in the substance tradition, Descartes invokes a new sort of stuff, mental substance, which houses the new entity. When Descartes says that the essence of mind is thought, he means just that – this essence is the intentional. There are two kinds of stuff because there are two kinds of property.[22]

We said above that Descartes, by his use of innate, intentional ideas, rules out alternative notions of semantics. In chapter 1 we described in some detail the early functionalist approach to semantics via an information problem. The classical answer to this problem from early modern philosophy invoked the theory of ideas. Descartes and Locke, its first champions, argued that, in light of the new science, there was a complex causal chain between object and mind that ended in the awareness of an idea or, as Dennett terms it, an internal representation. Internal representations are information carriers. Locke and Descartes spoke of them as if they represented objects to the mind, perhaps like pictures, or even language. Leaving the accuracy of this characterization aside for a moment, we can best see the structure of the theory of ideas by turning to Dennett's critique of ideas as information carriers. Dennett's view of internal representations revolves around regresses and circularities:

... I think AI has broken the back of an argument that has bedeviled philosophers and psychologists for over two hundred years. Here is a skeletal version of it: *First*, the only psychology that could possibly succeed in explaining the complexities of human activity must posit internal representations. This premise has been deemed obvious by just about everyone except the radical behaviorists (both in psychology and philosophy – both Watson and Skinner, and Ryle and

Malcolm). Descartes doubted almost everything but this. For the British Empiricists, the internal representations were called ideas, sensations, impressions; more recently psychologists have talked of hypotheses, maps, schemas, images, propositions, engrams, neural signals, even holograms and whole innate theories. So the first premise is quite invulnerable, or at any rate it has an impressive mandate. But, *second*, nothing is intrinsically a representation of anything; something is a representation only *for* or *to* someone; any representation or system of representations thus requires at least one *user* or *interpreter* of the representation who is external to it. Any such interpreter must have a variety of psychological or intentional traits: it must be capable of a variety of *comprehension*, and must have beliefs and goals (so it can *use* the representation to *inform* itself and thus assist it in achieving its goals). Such an interpreter is then a sort of homunculus.

Therefore, psychology *without* homunculi is impossible. But psychology *with* homunculi is doomed to circularity or infinite regress, so psychology is impossible.

The argument given is a relatively abstract version of a familiar group of problems. For instance, it seems (to many) that we cannot account for perception unless we suppose it provides us with an internal image (or model or map) of the external world, and yet what good would that image do us unless we have an inner eye to perceive it, and how are we to explain its capacity for perception? It also seems (to many) that understanding a heard sentence must be somehow *translating* it into some internal message, but how will this message in turn be understood: by translating it into something else?[23]

Exactly what are the alleged circularities and regresses? Dennett gives some examples in the quoted passage, claiming they 'are a relatively abstract version of a familiar group of problems.' Here, we offer what we take to be the keys to these abstract formulations. They fall into two groups.[24]

(1) *Semantic problems*: Internal representations are presumably caused by external objects. One thinks here, perhaps, of the internal representations of a Turing machine caused by pushing the keys on a keyboard. These representations are information carriers, but precisely what this means needs attention. It is not that someone looking at the representations assigns a semantics in the arbitrary way one might in constructing a logic or algebra. When one does that, one chooses a set of signs and rules for combining them and then assigns meanings to the signs by hooking them to a domain of objects. But in the case of the internal representations involved in sense perception, presumably the causes of the internal representations stand in specific relationships to them that we

need to discover, as it were. But how is one to read those interpretations for information? To do so, one needs to know how the objects or events that cause the representations stand with respect to one another and to the representations themselves. We need to know things about the causes which, unfortunately, the representations themselves are supposed to provide. If we do know the characteristics of the domain of objects, then we don't need representations.

(2) *Syntactic problems*: In addition to having to know the characteristics of the domain of objects, we also need to know the characteristics of the representors in order to understand their semantics. Representations have a 'syntax,' a set of characteristics, analogous to a language, which themselves must be grasped, or else their semantics cannot be understood. Interpreting representations means coordinating *their* characteristics with what they are about. Thus we *seem* to have a repeat of the original information problem, but now with representors instead of trees, as it were. Indeed, there are those in the seventeenth century – Foucher for one – who saw it that way.[25]

We believe that the Cartesian view of the mental, as well as Berkeley's (as we argue in a later chapter) is meant to *avoid* the semantic and syntactic problems. That is, there are metaphysical reasons why Descartes and Berkeley do not give up the theory of ideas in light of the obviousness of (1) and (2), above. Neither theological concerns nor philosophical blindness plays a role here.

In what sense are objects about which we get information external (to use Dennett's term) to, or outside of, the homunculus? This sense, if there is but one, is crucial, since it is this externality that generates the need for a representative to give information. Now this cannot be just an 'action at a physical distance' problem, or it would be solved by taking brain states as intermediaries. What Descartes sees is that the question of the relationship between the brain state and the perceptual experience of the tree presents a problem different from that of the *spatially* external tree. In speaking of the 'picture' on the back of the eye, he says: 'Now, when this picture thus passes to the inside of our heads, it still bears some resemblance to the objects from which it proceeds. As I have amply shown already, however, we must not think that it is by means of this resemblance that the picture causes our sensory perception of these objects – as if there were yet other eyes within our brain with which we could perceive it.'[26]

The physical process must come to an end. Suppose it ends in a brain state. We again are faced with the problem of how one gets information from the physical world, in this case, from the brain state. Descartes, we think, grasps this clearly; for him, it is a matter of the semantic problem. While it is not the object of a perceptual act involving the organs of sensation, the brain state cannot itself represent the physical object which gave rise to it without it being provided a specific representative function. Could the brain state be assigned such a function? Descartes, we think, sees that to do so would involve one of the problems described in (1), above. Therefore, some entity must be invested with an inherent representational power, and that representation must be grasped without need for an intermediary. That entity is the idea of the tree. Descartes sees that, given (1) and (2), the only way to solve the problems is to build a semantics into the idea, to make it intentional. He so characterizes ideas that their logical structure is different from the logic of ordinary things, as we have explained above.[27] Given this radically different logical structure, Descartes invokes direct acquaintance, where, by its very nature, one grasps the internal representation without intermediaries. Acts of direct acquaintance are not information gatherers; no intermediary is necessary for them to do their work. Of course, this means that, within seventeenth-century metaphysical constraints, ideas are now radically different sorts of things from any physical state or process.

Dennett dismisses the point about direct acquaintance; he doesn't allow that the homunculus scanning a representation can be so interpreted that (2) is blocked. But the Cartesian argument, after all, is (in effect) that we do manage to perceive, and how could we do that if (1) and (2) were true, and at the same time representations were unavoidable, unless there is an act that does not engender more representations? In this sense, it makes little difference whether one interprets Cartesian ideas as *properties* of acts of awareness, such as perceptions or beliefs, or *objects* of acts of direct awareness. Henceforth, we shall speak as if the Cartesian position is the latter, since, even if it is the former, it makes no difference to the structure of our argument.

To summarize: Descartes claims that sensible qualities, even sensed shapes, are not like what they supposedly represent, that the new science shows that the older view of something shared between the object and the perceptual state is naïve. But there is more to the Cartesian argument than a conclusion of mere *physical* unlikeness; if there were not, one might think that brain states, whose qualities are of the same kind as, but not literally the same as, the entities that cause them, would serve as the requisite information carriers. But they cannot so serve, simply because no physical entity has the requisite semantic properties to overcome the semantic problem discussed above. It is only if the representing entities are different in kind from the physical, that is, only if they are *intentional* and represent by their very nature, that the semantic problem can be overcome. It is not that sensible qualities cannot be like physical qualities because they are assumed for some reason to be ideas. They are taken to be ideas because they cannot serve their function of representation if they are merely physical qualities.[28]

We are now in a better position to evaluate the hypothesis that Descartes's ideas have a structure, like sense data. Several Cartesian doctrines go against this hypothesis. For one, describing sense data as having the logical structure expressed by, say, 'Fa' makes *a* into a logical subject, a substance. This would put Descartes, who is still a (somewhat modified) Aristotelian with respect to the substance doctrine,[29] in the untenable position of having momentary substances modifying minds, since, after all, ideas are modifications of mental substance. This point alone shows that a coherent 'way of ideas' theorist must carefully rethink the logical structure of ideas. Furthermore, under the hypothesis that perceptual ideas are sense data, to treat the sense datum like another *thing with physical properties* may seem to Descartes to invite the positing of another intermediary and another awareness to grasp it. That is, either the sense datum has the same sort of properties originally assigned to physical objects or it does not. If it does, we seem to have the same problem that calls for intermediaries as we originally had. So, under the view of non-intrinsic representation, the properties of the representation must be grasped by means of another representation in order for its perceiver to *assign* it a semantics. But there is, quite obviously, an additional issue. A theory of representations is faced with the problem of hooking them to the world. In the case of, say, interpreting a language, one usually considers that one has the world and the language, and coordinates the latter to the former. A theorist with representations to work with has only her counterpart of the latter. This is simply a version of the problem of the external world. As a necessary condition for our knowledge of that world, then, a theorist with representations needs a semantics that guarantees that they represent. No theory with representations having the structure of the things they represent can give that guarantee.

In short, if a sense datum has the same structure as that which it allegedly represents, it cannot be successfully used as a representation. To see this is already to take a giant step towards transforming sense data into genuinely intentional entities. That is, what properties a sense datum has is irrelevant; the crucial fact is that it must point to something beyond itself. The lesson is to treat representations with a very different logic than that of things, that is, intentionally. The great virtue of an intentional theory is that it solves an otherwise insoluble semantic problem. We argue below that, when seen correctly, Descartes's theory of the objective reality of ideas does just that.

One can see these points illustrated in Descartes's use of the primary–secondary quality distinction. The distinction between primary and secondary qualities calls for a radical change in the logic of ideas from that of having a subject–predicate structure. Descartes, of course, does not believe that colours, smells, and so on characterize anything in the physical world. What is their ontological status? Descartes here considers one of the major problems of the seventeenth century. His solution, as we understand it, is to deny colours the status of qualities of *anything*. Thus, colour percepts cannot be treated as later theorists treated sense data. The whole point of moving colours out of objects would become obscure, to say the least, if colours retained their status as properties. This point, however, is not confined to secondary qualities. If Descartes had given them the status of qualities, for example, of sense data somehow in the mind, what of those shape properties in ideas? We would surely have to grant them the same sort of status as qualities, thereby having primary qualities in minds in a most uncomfortable way.[30] Indeed, if such shape properties – in modern parlance, phenomenal shapes – characterize sense data, what is the relation of such properties to physical shape? However, if our argument is correct, it leaves not only shape percepts, but also colour percepts, with a structure which certainly sounds intentional, and surely, it could be argued, Descartes's discussion of material falsity shows that colour percepts are *not* intentional. We return to this important objection in the next chapter.

We have argued above that, in missing the simple–complex distinction, Danto fails to see why, for Descartes, ideas are capable of falsehood as well as truth. This failure on his part goes hand in hand with another: Danto never explains *why* Descartes holds that ideas are about something which is *guaranteed* to exist. We agree with Danto that Descartes makes this guarantee for what he and we have termed the 'simple constituents' of perceptual ideas. But unless one can show how Descartes forges this guarantee, the heart of Danto's point remains. We now shall show how Descartes conceives of the guarantee, and how this conception allows him to escape Danto's main criticism.

In his first proof for the existence of God in the Third Meditation, Descartes claims that the only conceivable cause for his idea of God must be a being with as much formal reality as his idea has objective reality. To say that the cause of his idea has this formal reality is to say that it has those properties which are presented in the idea of God. Descartes clearly ties this causal principle to what we call the *ex nihilo* principle: something cannot come from nothing.[31] For suppose that something that had none of the properties of God were the cause of our idea of God. Then it would be inexplicable, inconceivable, how the idea was produced by its cause. Of course, even with the *ex nihilo* principle operative, it may not exactly be crystal clear as to *how* God causes the idea in us of his properties. But this will be a mystery even if there *was ex nihilo* causation. *Ex nihilo* causation would add a second mystery.

The spectre of *ex nihilo* causation, we believe, drives much of the argumentation of the *Meditations*:

Now it is manifest by the natural light that there must be as least as much <reality> in the efficient and total cause as in the effect of that cause. For where, I ask, could the effect get its reality from, if not from the cause? And how could the cause give it to the effect unless it possessed it? It follows from this both that something cannot arise from nothing, and also that what is more perfect – that is, contains in itself more reality – cannot arise from what is less perfect. And this is transparently true not only in the case of effects which possess <what philosophers call> actual or formal reality, but also in the case of ideas, where one is considering only <what they call> objective reality. A stone, for example, which previously did not exist, cannot begin to exist unless it is produced by something which contains, either formally or eminently, everything to be found in the stone; similarly, heat cannot be produced in an object which was not previously hot, except by something of at least the same order <degree or kind> of perfection as heat, and so on. But it is also true that the idea of heat, or of a stone, cannot exist in me unless it is put there by some cause which contains at least as much reality as I conceive to be in the heat or in the stone. For although this cause does not transfer any of its actual or formal reality to my idea, it should not on that account be supposed that it must be less real. The nature of an idea is such that of itself it requires no formal reality except what it derives from my thought, of which it is a mode. But in order for a given idea to contain such and such objective reality, it must surely derive it from some cause which contains at least as much formal reality as there is objective reality in the idea. For if we suppose that an idea contains something that was not in its cause, it must have got this from nothing; yet the mode of being by which a thing exists objectively <or

representatively> in the intellect by way of an idea, imperfect though it may be, is certainly not nothing, and so it cannot come from nothing.[32]

As we shall explain it, Descartes's application of the *ex nihilo* principle to the origin in us of the idea of God illustrates one way (but as we shall see, not the only way) that he uses this principle in the *Meditations*. Although, in the quotation, Descartes mentions the notion of efficient cause, it is not an accident that he also invokes the notion of *formal* reality. An efficient cause is, so to speak, the energy which produces the effect, or the idea, but there are constraints on what a cause must be like to do this. This echo of the Aristotelian idea of formal cause will be important to our later discussion. Just as our ordinary belief about our perceptions of physical objects is that the causes of these perceptions are identical to what they present, so Descartes's claim about the idea of God is that its cause is identical to its content. If there were something in the content that was not in the cause, where would this content come from? But now imagine a situation in which a powerful being places in our minds *other* ideas, ideas that are *not* identical to her properties, that is, as some have imagined, ideas of a physical world. Here, too, we shall argue that the *ex nihilo* principle applies. This sort of case brings us to the 'evil demon' hypothesis and its connection to the principle.

3

The Secularity of the *Meditations*

It is fruitful, we think, to see the denial of the *ex nihilo* principle as equivalent to the 'evil demon' hypothesis. For what is the threat of the evil demon? Precisely that the reality that our simple ideas present to us fails to correspond to the world as it is. Now, if a demon were causing our ideas in such a way that they seemed to represent what they did not, which is the case if nothing exists that matches up to what the idea presents, Descartes's fears would be realized. His fears, however, are more complex than they appear.

As we see it, the so-called 'evil demon' hypothesis is actually a series of hypotheses concerning distinct but related problems. Each of these hypotheses envisions systematic doubt, and each is driven by the same logic. Even the dream problem, which seems on its face distinct from the demon hypotheses, can be interpreted as following the systematic pattern of the demons. There is, first of all, the possibility that all our ordinary judgments about physical objects and the relations between them are mistaken: there is a physical world, but it is not what we think it is. There is, second, the possibility that there is no physical world at all, but merely, if we can put it this way, a set of possible worlds from which the demon creates in us the false belief that we are in contact with an actual world. There is, third, a most insidious world in which our ideas are not at all what they seem; we only – in some confused way – *believe* we know what they present to us. That is, we believe that we know, on the basis of our ideas, what the world would be like if those representations were to be instantiated. But, on the hypothesis of the existence of the third demon, we would be mistaken about what the world would be like if those representations were instantiated. Here, we are alone with the demon, or, as we shall now explain this possibility, as alone as a logical atom. We shall argue that the exorcism of this last demon is a presupposition for the intelligibility of the other two, and that the Third Meditation shows this. We shall first introduce a sketch of our interpretation of the Third Meditation or, more accurately, what we believe that Descartes *ought* to have said in that meditation, given the later work 'Comments on a Certain Broadsheet.' It is our view that, on the basis of what he says in 'Comments on a Certain Broadsheet,' a fully consistent semantics for ideas can be constructed which does not lead him to circularity. We will provide details of our argument by contrasting our view with Margaret Wilson's. We conclude the chapter by developing some further ideas on the crucial concepts of *ex nihilo* causation and eminent containment.

Let us begin with the idealized version of the Third Meditation: That *all* simple ideas have objective reality is its central tenet. As we explicated the notion of objective reality in chapter 2, to say an idea has objective reality is in effect to say that it presents the conditions for the exemplification of its constituent(s);[1] that we know, in other words, what the world would have to be like for our ideas to represent. Descartes introduces the notion of objective reality in the Third Meditation because he intends to demonstrate that ideas must be intrinsically *meaningful*. This demonstration allows him to reach the central goal of the Third Meditation: to escape the circle of ideas, to show that something exists besides himself and his ideas. The introduction of the *ex nihilo* principle in fact provides that escape by providing a semantic rule for ideas: the objective reality of an idea takes us to a world beyond ideas and the mind that has them.

The nature of an idea is such that of itself it requires no formal reality except what it derives from my thought, of which it is a mode. But in order for a given idea to contain such and such objective reality, it must surely derive it from some cause which contains at least as much formal reality as there is objective reality in the idea. For if we suppose that an idea contains something which was not in its cause, it must have got this from nothing; yet the mode of being by which a thing exists objectively in the intellect by way of an idea, imperfect though it may be, is certainly not nothing, and so cannot come from nothing.

And although the reality which I am considering in my ideas is merely objective reality, I must not on that account suppose that the same reality need not exist formally in the causes of my ideas, but that it is enough for it to be present in them objectively. For just as the objective mode of being belongs to ideas by their very nature, so the formal mode of being belongs to the causes of ideas – or at least the first and most important ones – by *their* very nature. And although one idea may perhaps originate from another, there cannot be an infinite regress here; eventually one must reach a primary idea, the cause of which will be like an archetype which contains formally <and in fact> all the reality <or perfection> which is present only objectively <or representatively> in the idea.[2]

Taking the *ex nihilo* principle seriously, it certainly appears that we immediately escape the circle of ideas; ideas of qualities like shapes, for example, would *seem* to require causes outside of themselves and outside of us. But matters are not so simple, for, after claiming that all ideas have objective reality, Descartes *appears* to take it back. First and foremost, he claims that we could be the causes of our own ideas of shapes and other mathematical qualities in the sense that we could *eminently contain* such qualities. 'As for all the other elements which make up the ideas of corporeal things, namely extension, shape, position and movement, these are not formally contained in me since I am nothing but a thinking thing; but since they are merely modes of a substance, and I am a substance, it seems possible that they are contained in me eminently.'[3] As we understand it (we discuss eminent containment in much more detail later in this chapter), X eminently contains Y if it has the *power* to produce either Y or an idea of Y. *Prima facie*, eminent containment appears to violate the *ex nihilo* principle, so that Descartes's claims about the causation of ideas are not consistent with that principle. Second, in his introduction of the notion of material falsity, he appears to add a further complication – an idea may appear to have objective reality, and yet may fail to do so.

We shall show that the doctrine of material falsity raises some of the same problems as the possible eminent containment of ideas of primary qualities by the self that thinks them – namely, that our ideas could present us with bogus, not genuine, possibilities. Furthermore, we argue in detail below that the possibility of error could not arise unless we understood the *meaning* of the ideas presented, what they are about. These meanings, as we later argue, are provided by innate ideas whose semantics in turn involves us with a theory of exemplars. Descartes's claims in 'Comments on a Certain Broadsheet' puts the doctrine of the material falsity of the ideas of secondary qualities into proper logical perspective. All ideas of primary and secondary qualities are innate, and the semantics of innate ideas is critical for the escape from the circle of ideas. In other words, by the time Descartes writes 'Comments on a Certain Broadsheet' he realizes that, in order to solve the information problem, that is, to provide ideas with a proper semantics, he must accept the innateness of the ideas of both primary and secondary qualities.

We shall argue, further, that there is a sense in which Descartes's premise that he himself could be the cause of all his ideas of sense in both the Third and the Sixth Meditations is disingenuous. Not only does he give rather weak reasons in the latter for dismissing himself as the possible cause of the ideas in question – his passivity and so on – but he need only to have appealed to his own doctrine of eminent containment to escape the circle. As we shall show, far from raising the strong possibility that all ideas of sense are caused by one's own self, the doctrine of eminent containment, when properly explicated, erases that possibility. Descartes, in other words, has in the Third Meditation given all the machinery he needs to escape the circle of ideas – in this case, the third demon – without turning to God. The *Meditations* is not circular but secular.

To defend our view that all simple ideas have objective reality, we turn first to the third demon. To illustrate this demon's power, we consider the views of Margaret Wilson, who, in effect, interprets Descartes's discussion of material falsity and objective reality to show that what we call 'the demon' is unwittingly Descartes himself. To repeat, the problem of the third demon is this: We might believe that we know what the world would be like if the properties our ideas represent were instantiated (to know what the world would be like is to speak of a possible world), and yet be mistaken. It is not that we think our ideas have content when they do not; it is, rather, that the content we think they have is not their content at all. Thus, for example, one might believe that if one has a red idea, the possible world that idea represents is one in which red is instantiated; but if the demon is at large, the possible world that idea represents might be one in which blue were the property exemplified. Even worse, it might be that red is not instantiated *in any possible world.* In either case, one would be mistaken about what one believes is the content of one's own ideas – one believes that the idea presents something which it does not. In such a world we would not know the *meaning* of our own ideas, for knowing the meaning of our thoughts and ideas is, at the very least, knowing what properties are presented by them, that is, knowing what an instantiation of such a property would be like.

Wilson's discussion of material falsity invokes these ideas about both real and vacant possibilities.

In fact, when Descartes asks whether or not his ideas are of 'certain things' he is *not* raising the question whether they represent to him entities that actually exist.

For he indicates very explicitly, in both the *Meditations* and the *Principles*, that what represents *res* and what does not, depends on a concept of reality that is not equivalent to existence. For instance, he says a little later in the Third Meditation that 'although perhaps it is possible to imagine that such a being [as God] does not exist, it is nevertheless not possible to imagine that his idea exhibits nothing real to me.' Several texts strongly suggest that when Descartes asks whether an idea represents something real, or *rem*, he is asking whether or not in some way it gives him cognizance of a *possible* existant.[4]

Wilson now asks whether materially false ideas present such possibilities, and answers that, in Descartes's view, they do not. She concludes from this negative answer that, contrary to what he said previously, Descartes does not believe all ideas have objective reality. In anticipation of this conclusion, she has already distinguished between what she calls the 'representational' character of an idea and its objective reality. A materially false idea has representational character but lacks objective reality. On the basis of Third Meditation passages,[5] she claims that, for Descartes, *all* ideas have representational character. They 'are received by the mind *as if exhibiting to it* various things – or as if making things *cognitively accessible.*'[6] The question is, why do not materially false ideas – colour ideas or, more generally, all ideas of so-called secondary qualities – then have objective reality?

We need a clearly defined notion of objective reality. In Wilson's view, an idea has objective reality only if it presents a genuine possibility. Why do not materially false ideas present such possibilities? According to Wilson,

As Descartes ... explains to Arnauld, to say an idea is materially false is to say that it provides 'material' for falsity in the strict sense, or formal reality: i.e., it tends to lead its unwary possessor into making false judgments ... If 'in fact' light, colour, heat, cold and so forth are 'nothing real' or 'non things' [*nullas res*], the ideas that represent these 'qualities' as if they were real [*tanquam res*] are to this extent materially false. In other words, the fact that an idea has representational character – that it presents itself *as if* exhibiting some thing to the mind, or making it cognitively accessible – leads us falsely to suppose that it does make something real cognitively accessible to us ...[7]

In the continuation of [his] account of ideas of sense, however, Descartes gives a peculiar twist to the story of how they are caused. There is no reason, he remarks, to suppose at this stage of his inquiry that these 'obscure' ideas have causes outside himself.[8]

There is apparent trouble here for the *ex nihilo* principle. If it is true in general that something cannot come from nothing, in the ways which we have described above, in what sense do colours come from us? Perhaps we eminently contain them? Wilson does not explicitly entertain this possibility. She interprets Descartes as claiming that materially false ideas need no cause, they arise from a defect in our nature; even if such ideas were true, Descartes claims, they are so obscure that they could arise from our own being. Wilson concludes, with seeming justification, that although such ideas have representational character, they have no objective reality. For, after all, if they had objective reality they would need a cause which has formally or eminently as much reality as the effect has objectively. Something with 'no cause' can have no such objective reality, and it is certainly not clear how, if one is the cause of one's ideas of secondary qualities, one could still maintain the 'objective reality' doctrine with respect to them. Even if it were clear, Descartes is worrying the question of whether anything exists besides himself. If he is the formal cause of all his ideas, so that the objective–formal reality distinction can be maintained, this does not move us out of the sphere of one's own ideas.[9]

This conclusion about materially false ideas bodes ill for Descartes. Why can't *other* ideas merely *seem* to have objective reality, since they will have representational character? Even clear and distinct ideas, which Wilson earlier had cited as a criterion for the presentation of real possibilities, will not help here, since Descartes raises the possibility that even they could be caused by one's own mental substance. Thus the third demon has reared a very ugly head – it now seems possible that all our ideas could merely have representational character, presenting us with only apparent possibilities. For every such idea, we would have the belief that it presents something it does not present.

Something is amiss here. Wilson's Descartes certainly has difficulties. To address them, we need to consider more closely what it means to say that ideas are presented 'as if of things.' When Descartes says that ideas are 'as if of things,' there is a crucial ambiguity which leads to two different notions of material falsity. (1) He may, and seemingly does sometimes, mean this from the philosopher's point of view; the philosopher, or at least Descartes, knows that what we are directly aware of in sense experience are our own ideas. Ideas may or may not *represent* actually existing things in the physical world. The philosopher claims that, since they are mere ideas and not the things they are about, they present us *at best* with mere possibilities; *at best*, we know what would be the case if they were true. An idea of perception that one has now of a square thing does indeed present a possibility even if there happens to be no exemplification of square at that moment. We recall Wilson's example of the idea of God, quoted above, in which Descartes claims that, even if there is no God, we must recognize that God is a possible entity, that the idea presents some reality to us. The situation is different with the ideas of secondary qualities, at least according to Descartes. The concept of material falsity is introduced to handle these cases. A materially false idea of red only appears to present a possibility, but in fact it presents no possibility at all. Of course one may ask, as we do shortly, how an idea can merely *appear* to present a possibility. An idea that presented us with no possibilities would be uncomfortably similar to a logical contradiction, such as thinking of a round square. In the case of round squares, we might say today that there is no possible world in which they exist. But Descartes does not think of ideas of secondary qualities as contradictory in this sense, even if they are confused. Thus, when Wilson claims that red ideas do not present us with possibilities, we seem to have, at least in a modern sense, an unexplicated sense of 'possibility.' As we suggest shortly, it may be precisely because Descartes comes to realize that he has an unexplicated sense of 'possibility' with secondary qualities and that he finally assigns a semantics to such ideas.

(2) There is another way, however, to interpret the claim that all ideas are 'as if of things.' The *ordinary person* believes that his perceptual idea of red is actually a presentation of a red thing, and not an idea at all. It is not as if the ordinary person thinks he is presented with a possibility which may not be actualized; he thinks he is presented with the actuality itself. So, 'as if of things' means 'exactly like seeing the thing as it is.' Neither a red nor a square presentation presents us with something *else*, something these ideas are *about*. This changes our understanding of the nature of the mistake made with respect to materially false ideas. The mistake is to confuse what we, ordinary perceivers, *understand* to be the case, and what is the case, since, again, there are no red things. Here, as we shall argue, since we understand something to be the case, there is something to be understood; thus we can keep the view that all ideas have objective reality, even if some are materially false.

We wish now to explicate more fully the connection between (1) and (2).

When one assesses why the ordinary person makes the mistake in (2) – the mistake of judging something true that is materially false – the answer is revelatory. For the ordinary perceiver, seeing a red thing is exactly like seeing a square thing, in the sense that we are presented with a property that appears to be instantiated; there is no intrinsic difference for us between the two situations (as Berkeley forcefully points out). From Descartes's point of view, however, the ordinary person does not even know what it would be like to see a red thing; there is nothing that seeing a red thing is like. That is the point of (1). Even though we *think* we understand what the world is like when we have a red sensation, we are wrong: the world is mathematical in character and so we are not really understanding anything at all about the world of square things when we believe, say, that the square thing is red. What we can visualize and what is the case may well be two completely different things. This is precisely what Berkeley later disputes; for him, what is (at least) visually imaginable is possible. For Descartes, however, the visual is not necessarily the possible. This is one reason why he characterizes ideas of secondary qualities as confused. They are confused because we think, mistakenly from a philosopher's point of view, that there are properties when in fact these are not properties at all.

Unfortunately for Descartes, there are philosophical pressures to yield to the philosopher's sense of 'as if of things.' The oddity of his claim with respect to (2), which illustrates the ambiguity of the phrase 'as if of things' is that there is no intrinsic difference between the situation of seeing a red thing, which Descartes finds inherently confused, and seeing a square one, which he finds quite intelligible.[10] There is a conflict between (1) and the facts of the ordinary perceiver's situation. While (1) leads us to think that some ideas have no objective reality, (2) requires a *ground* for the similarity between true ideas (e.g., 'This is square') and materially false ideas (e.g., 'This is red'). There must be something about the presentations that makes them similar, that makes them 'as if of things' in the sense that the ordinary perceiver thinks there is a red thing or a square thing before her. The identification of this ground, which does not occur until the publication of 'Comments on a Certain Broadsheet,' yields the view that Descartes first espouses in the Third Meditation, that all ideas do have objective reality. It is not that Descartes wants to say that there is a red thing and a square thing – for there is nothing of which 'is red' is true. Rather, to ground the meaning of 'as if of things' in (2), he must claim that both red ideas and square ideas point to something beyond themselves.[11]

Does Descartes hold both (1) and (2), that is, two different views of material falsity? The strain shows in what Wilson calls 'representational character.' Believing that Descartes must distinguish between objective reality and representational character because of the 'material falsity' problem, she explicates the notion of representational character with Descartes's view that *all ideas are as if of things*. But, as we have shown, the italicized phrase is ambiguous. In the sense of (1), an idea may have representational character yet be materially false, and thus not present any possibility. In the sense of (2), the same idea may have representational character, be materially false, and yet present a possibility. We believe that, in the *Meditations*, Descartes vacillates between these two positions, only resolving the problem with his introduction, in 'Comments on a Certain Broadsheet,' of the claim that colour ideas are innate.[12] Innate ideas, as we discuss at length later in this chapter, have a semantics involving exemplars, so that we at last have the entities whose formal reality grounds the objective reality of ideas. It is clear, however, that, in the *Meditations*, Wilson is right: Descartes explicitly embraces (1). Yet, if Wilson is right, he maintains that all ideas are 'as if of things' (have representational character) without the *ground* for that claim that objective reality would provide. In sense (1), an idea presents something beyond itself, something the idea *means*. To say an idea has objective reality is to point to something beyond the idea which gives the idea its content, what it means. Without the notion of objective reality to ground representational character, in what sense can an idea *be* 'as if of a thing'? Surely, again, not in sense (1); and sense (1) lets in the third demon. It is because all ideas are 'as if of things' in sense (2) that Descartes may believe he can avoid the 'third demon' problem in the *Meditations*; representational character saves him, not because he embraces (1), but because he sometimes thinks that 'all ideas are as if of things,' as in (2). As we have seen, the sense in (2) is compatible with all ideas having objective reality.

One might argue that we have not shown that there is sufficient similarity in alternative (2) between red presentations and square presentations to insist on a ground for that similarity. The apparent logical grammar, to use an analogy, of 'The present king of France is bald' is subject–predicate, but it is not really subject–predicate; so by analogy the apparent logical grammar of 'This is red' is predicative, but it is not. Or 'Quadruplicity drinks procrastination' seems like subject–verb–object, but it is a category error of some kind. The problem with these analogies is that they are too strong for the case of secondary qualities. 'The present king of France is bald' leads to logical difficulties; 'This is red' does not so lead. Any speaker of English knows there is something wrong with 'Quadruplicity ...,' but the ordinary person does not see anything wrong with attributing colours to objects. The problem with attributing colours to the physical world is not logical or grammatical. This, of course, is one of the oddities that is presented to us by the attempt to make the distinction between primary and secondary qualities. Descartes, we think, resolves this within his system perfectly. Given the theory of innate ideas promulgated in 'Comments on a Certain Broadsheet,' Descartes recognizes that there is a sense in which coloured things are possible, even if not physically possible in this world. Innate ideas, after all, cannot be semantically messy.

We must take care to distinguish the third demon from the first two described above. Unless we understand our own ideas in the sense that they present us with genuine possibilities, the very ground of intelligibility for doubting the existence of a physical world or for a demon causing us to believe that a statement about that world is true, when it is really false, would be lost. Nor could the first and second demons be overcome. If our thoughts could mean something other than we believe they mean, then no proof for the actual existence of anything, including God and the *cogito*, could give us results. This is not a matter of clarity and distinctness, but a matter of understanding what it is that is clear and distinct. However, it is true that, once we exorcise the third demon, we also exorcise the need for a proof for the existence of God to get beyond our own ideas. Once we know there is a ground for the meaningfulness of our ideas, we are beyond the circle of ideas *if* we can also show – as we do below – that we could not eminently contain the causes of all our own ideas.

Why claim that Descartes *wants* to or sees that he must avoid the third demon? Certainly in the Third Meditation, he does not see or avoid the third demon in any clear way. As Wilson has argued, he seems to opt for sense (1), above, of the phrase 'all ideas are as if of things' which yields trouble – ultimately, the circularity of the *Meditations*. We have shown, however, that there are grounds for claiming that Descartes, even if unclear, sees that he needs the view that all ideas have objective reality to have any hope of escaping the circle of ideas. The evidence in the *Meditations* is his vacillation between the view that all ideas have objective reality and some do not; his implicit jumps between (1) and (2) which parallel that vacillation; and finally the implicit claim (pointed out clearly by Wilson) that the 'material falsity' doctrine is a red herring anyway, given that he entertains the possibility that even ideas of primary qualities are caused by the self.[13] If that were true, all ideas could still have objective reality and yet be caused by the person having the ideas, perhaps – as we discuss shortly – eminently contained by the self.[14] The concept of representational character, introduced by Wilson, perfectly demonstrates Descartes's uneasiness. His claim in 'Comments on a Certain Broadsheet' provides the final step in his semantic theory. When he claims there that even colour ideas are innate, he recognizes their intelligibility and thus that they present us with possibilities. For innate ideas have a semantics and are connected with what we have termed 'exemplars'; these exemplars are the ground of meaningfulness of innate ideas. No longer are colour ideas assigned to a defect in our character; they simply are not denizens of this actual world. With the semantics of ideas of secondary qualities in place, Descartes has in effect rendered the *Meditations* thus amended (and with the caveat on eminent containment issued above) into a treatise on secular semantics.

The Cartesian answer to the third demon, that all ideas must be meaningful, have objective reality, is reminiscent of a fatal criticism of the positivistic doctrine of verificationism. For the verificationist, to say a sentence is meaningful is to say that there are possible states of affairs which verify it. If there are no such states, the sentence is meaningless. But the anti-verificationist reply, analogous in structure to ours, is simply that we could not know what states of affairs were possible verifiers unless we know what the sentence means.

Thus, to take Wilson's construction, an idea must present a genuine possibility in order to have objective reality. When one perceives a colour, according to the *Meditations*, one is not perceiving a genuine possibility. The 'demon' problem would allow a separation between being presented with red and knowing what a *possible* world would be like if red were instantiated. Yet, if we were not in some sense considering a possibility, how could the idea's representational character fool us into making the error of believing there are red things? [15] Whatever the verifier of the idea turns out to be, the demon could not have fun at one's expense unless one was fooled about something. One is fooled because one believes that a certain state of affairs would verify the idea, when it in fact does not. So in order to be fooled, we must understand something – namely, what would be true if our (mistaken) belief were true.

Thus, there can be no mere *appearance* of meaning; some appearances cannot be deceiving. The issue is not whether there are any things which exist with the property F, let us say, but how we manage to envision the possibility that there are. If the idea of F has no meaning, in the sense of the intentional we outlined in chapter 2, what would we be envisioning when we believed that something was F? If such ideas were not meaningful, we couldn't be fooled into thinking there are, say, red things when in fact there are not. The *ex nihilo* principle as a constraint on efficient causality requires that the *meaningfulness* of ideas have an intentional structure such that a complex of such ideas *necessitates* which possibilities must be actualized in order for the ideas to be true; there are necessary connections between ideas and their intentions. An atomistic world, in which there are no such necessary connections because ideas are just things among things, would have ideas be meaningful in a totally different way. Any meaningfulness they have would be derivative, a function of their relationships to other entities. In such a view, it is not merely that the truth conditions for the ideas might not be actualized. Rather, ideas thought of atomistically in and of themselves have no truth conditions. This, indeed, was the point of our earlier argument about the representational possibilities of sense data.[16] We believe that Descartes gives ideas an intentional structure because he realizes that sense data or any other entities that must be *assigned* a semantics lead to insoluble difficulties. In this sense of 'assigned,' it makes no difference whether the assignment is made causally, as the functionalists do, or by coordinating each idea with something else. Neither can *guarantee* that, because our ideas are meaningful, there must be a world beyond them.[17] Extrinsically representational ideas could not even present us with the *possibility* of deception unless the intrinsic sense were presupposed. For why would one ever think there was a world beyond ideas which required us to assign a semantics to ideas, unless we had some notion of the intentional in the Cartesian sense?[18]

Our point, then, comes to the following: Even false ideas still have a sense, and this sense must come from somewhere – that is what the *ex nihilo* principle guarantees. Ontologically, there must be something that this intentional structure reflects. To deny this is to violate what we take to be the *ex nihilo* principle for the causes of ideas; the *meaning* of the idea cannot come from nothing.[19] There has to be something that grounds it: not the fact that there is something that exemplifies the idea, but something that makes the idea *intelligible*. If we take the *ex nihilo* principle seriously, then even if we cite a mere Humean correlation, say, a brain state, with the idea in question, there must be an ontological ground for that correlation. The content cannot just pop into existence. If this argument is correct, even an all-powerful and evil genius could not create our ideas in us *ex nihilo*. One might believe, for example, that such a demon could create in us ideas that appear intentional but in fact are connected to nothing. But in order to deceive us, such a genius would have to have an idea of what meanings he wished to fool us about. Those ideas would then provide the very models, the very meanings, of our ideas. If the demon could create seemingly meaningful ideas in us without such ideas, we would have a truly irrational world, one that goes beyond even a Humean world where – contrary to the *ex nihilo* principle – there can be connections between cause and effect which are not necessary. In a world that features agent causation, in which only the will of a demon creates – a will not describable by its intentions, for that would involve the demon's ideas, and so not be *ex nihilo* in the relevant sense – there are not even constant conjunctions between causes and effects.[20]

One might argue that overturning the third demon depends upon the view that Humean or agent causation will not satisfy Descartes. But, the objection goes, there is considerable evidence that he believes God can create *ex nihilo*. Descartes's view of the powers of God threatens to overturn our secular analysis. There is a large controversy in the literature over the powers of the Christian god as conceived by Descartes.[21] He specifically argues that God creates at least some eternal truths, and perhaps therefore the exemplars or essences connected by these truths, *ex nihilo*, thus raising the possibility that God is totally exempt from the requirements of the *ex nihilo* principle. The case Descartes gives, from the Replies to the Sixth Set of Objections, is that the three angles of a triangle are equal to two right angles because God *wills* that they be, and not because they are necessarily so.[22] Indeed, it is God's will that makes it so. This example alone does not show that God creates *ex nihilo* the simple natures which are joined in this theorem; however, let us assume for the sake of the argument that he does. Perhaps, then, God can cause our ideas the same way he causes exemplars; perhaps tomorrow he will suspend the *ex nihilo* principle itself, even in those areas where Descartes thinks it applies.

However, we do not believe any of these situations is a threat to our view of Cartesian semantics. For one thing, even if Descartes claims that God creates exemplars *ex nihilo*, it does not follow that God can create *our* ideas that way. For another, the *ex nihilo* principle can be seen not as just another principle among principles, but, for Descartes, as the basis of rationality itself.

The common circularity charge against Descartes is that he needs God to be a non-deceiver in order to guarantee that the clarity and distinctness of a certain subset of his ideas give us truth. Given that we have broken the 'demon' problem into three distinct cases, the circularity charge must be correspondingly reinterpreted. In the current case, the issue is whether we need the goodness of God to guarantee that ideas have meaning. In our view, however, the question is not one of God's goodness, but rather of the world's rationality. What we are maintaining is that God *cannot* be a deceiver, not that he simply chooses to be otherwise. To put the point another way, we are claiming that the following situation is impossible: that God render the *ex nihilo* principle false, but out of his goodness simply makes it that, as a matter of fact, our ideas correctly present us with the situation that would obtain were the properties which are their content to be exemplified. For if it were out of his goodness, then it would be possible that he creates our ideas in the manner of agent causation described above. But, as we have argued, this possibility makes no sense to Descartes: it invokes a notion of semantics that involves us either in sense data (which falls to semantic regress) or the functionalist view (which presents us with no reasonable sense of truth conditions) of representations. The sceptical problem can be viewed as follows: There is a mind (our own) and a demon who, without plan, puts ideas in our heads in an order that seems to make sense to us. Secularized, the problem is that one could be a mind with a random series of thoughts generated in it, which thoughts seem to make sense, like the famous monkeys that produce *Hamlet*, but which in fact have no connection whatever to anything beyond them except Humean causation. Our point, which we believe is Descartes's, is that, if the order seems to make sense, that sense must be a function of the sense of its members. There can be, as we argued above, no mere appearance of meaning and, for there to be genuine meaning, ideas must be connected to exemplars (in ways we are in the midst of trying to describe). Thus, the *ex nihilo* principle is a constraint on God's power. Even if, as some think, Descartes's God can create contradictions, the *ex nihilo* principle must apply with respect to meaning. We could not even *form* a contradiction unless the principle were in place.

We have claimed that the doctrine of exemplars is a mainstay of Descartes's theory of meaning.[23] To use an analogy, exemplars are to ideas as essences are to Aristotelian substances – necessary connections are involved. The very nature of an idea is to be about something; what it is about stands to the idea like an essence stands to a substance. But Descartes says little about exemplars explicitly. We shall now argue that they are strongly implied in his discussion of formal and objective reality and, what goes with it, the doctrine of eminent containment.

Descartes's causal principle when applied to ideas is not merely that an idea's objective reality must be caused by a being that has at least as much formal reality, but that it may be caused by an entity that contains that thing *eminently.* As mentioned earlier in this chapter, eminent containment appears to violate the *ex nihilo* principle, so that Descartes's claims about the causation of ideas are not consistent with that principle: X eminently contains Y if it has the *power* to produce either Y or an idea of Y.[24] The problem is this: Y can produce an idea of Y by virtue of its formal reality. But X does not have to have that formal reality, merely the power to produce it, so how can X produce an idea of Y without violating the *ex nihilo* principle? That eventuality would have grave consequences for our view. For if *ex nihilo* causation is possible, scepticism again threatens, and a rational Cartesian semantics falls.

In order to assess this threat properly, we must try to get a clearer grasp of what exactly *ex nihilo* causation would be. Perhaps a mundane example will help. Suppose we meet a person who appears to be building a house. We say to her, 'That's a nice plan you are carrying out.' She replies that she has no plan. We ask her what architectural magazines she has been reading, and she replies that she has never seen such a magazine. We discover about the woman that she has never before seen a building and never before seen tools. The more such information we gather about her, the more incredulous we would become. That incredulity is, of course, precisely the point. That she could create a building from no plan, no previous ideas of buildings, no previous knowledge of what tools are or how they work, strikes us as impossible. Surely she possessed ideas on which her current activity rests. Notice that the principle that something cannot come from nothing is not satisfied merely by there being a cause for some effect. If what the woman tells us is true, and if she is building a building, she *might* (with some reluctance) be considered its cause. However, as we understand the *ex nihilo* principle from Descartes's use of it, the principle doesn't call merely for a cause of, say, an idea, but a particular *sort* of cause. We post-Humeans might wish to say the woman had the power to produce the building (after all, she did produce it), but we don't think Descartes would agree. *In such a case, he would look for a hidden variable. Descartes, in other words, would not take the sheer power to produce something as a proper explication of eminent containment.*

The doctrine of eminent containment, as we understand it, is part of Descartes's inheritance of causal principles, motivated by worries about the character of the Deity. If God creates extension, does it follow that God is extended? Not if God contains extension eminently, for then he is not characterized by extension, extension is not one of his properties. But if extension is not one of God's properties, so that he does not contain extension formally, how does God create extended things? Is it *ex nihilo*, as in the case suggested above? That case also suggests an answer. The most obvious explication of eminent containment of extension in this instance is either that God contains the *idea* of extension or, as another alternative goes, that he creates corporeal things from exemplars or archetypes which are not necessarily extended and which are in some sense independent of him. If God contains extension eminently, then he creates it, as it were, from his own ideas or from these external 'models.' Of course, there is a problem here. In the straightforward application of the *ex nihilo* principle, a physical cause which exemplifies a property F causes another event to have property F. An exemplar, seemingly, does not exemplify the property it is said to 'cause'; otherwise, what is the point of the appeal to eminent containment? Yet, Descartes waffles on this point. This Platonic problem of whether a model must share properties with what is modelled is, of course, not something peculiar to Cartesian metaphysics. We return to this problem shortly. First, we must try to draw some conclusions from the above discussion for the causation of ideas.

The lesson from Descartes's discussion of eminent containment is that exemplars are necessary to flesh out the full *ex nihilo* principle. Although the doctrine of eminent containment was, as we explained above, motivated by worries about the properties of God, we earlier invoked exemplars in a very different context – namely, to explain the ground for the intrinsic intentionality of ideas.[25] The innate idea of, say, triangle is not triangular and, if its cause is an exemplar, that cause may not exemplify the property of triangularity either.[26]

To put the point a bit differently, Descartes's doctrine of eminent containment, rather than being simply an obscure remnant of medieval philosophy, is crucial for understanding his theory of objective and formal reality of ideas. The meaning of an idea must have a ground. Just as one can use an idea to draw a model of a house, where neither the idea nor the model shares house-like properties with the house (at least, not in any clear way), one can have an idea, say, triangle 'from' an idea – an archetype or exemplar – without either sharing properties with a physical instantiation of triangle or being triangular. If we are correct, Descartes has extended the normal range of the *ex nihilo* principle beyond 'ordinary' efficient causation. The extension of the principle allows him to escape the demon of meaning without needing the goodness of God – a secular escape from the threat of circularity. What Descartes has done is to use the notion of 'formal ' in two different ways with respect to the *ex nihilo* principle. Straightforwardly, if the cause of an X exemplifies X itself, then the cause contains at least as much formal reality as the effect. If the cause of an X, or even of an idea of an X, is an exemplar of X, then the exemplar may be said to be the formal cause of the X, or the cause of the idea of the X. So the exemplar does not contain X formally, but is the formal cause none the less (thus invoking a notion close to the traditional, Aristotelian idea of formal cause). Eminent containment, then, is a way of keeping the notion of formal containment by extending it to the more traditional notion of formal cause.

There is another aspect of the problem of eminent containment, however, that must be explored before we can fully understand how God eminently contains the cause of corporeal things. Descartes claims in the Third Meditation that there is an ontological hierarchy – for example, substances are higher than modes – and that something higher in the hierarchy can cause something lower. Now, to say that, for example, a mind can cause some of its own ideas does not *prima facie* involve the notion of eminent containment: a mind could contain the formal cause of some of its own ideas in the straightforward sense that the mind or some of its contents might exemplify X and cause an idea of X. But when Descartes entertains the possibility in the Third Meditation that he is the cause of his own ideas of extension, eminent containment, as we shall now show, does play a role. In seeing that role, we shall see once again why a proper explication of eminent containment does not violate the *ex nihilo* principle.

In the Third Meditation, Descartes writes:

For just as the objective mode of being belongs to ideas by their very nature, so the formal mode of being belongs to the causes of ideas – or at least the first and most important ones – by *their* very nature. And although one idea may perhaps originate from another, there cannot be an infinite regress here; eventually one must reach a primary idea, the cause of which will be like an archetype which contains formally <and in fact> all the reality <or perfection> which is present only objectively <or representatively> in the idea.[27]

What is the principle Descartes wishes to defend here? According to the *ex nihilo* principle, the cause of an idea of X must be something that either formally exemplifies X or is an X-exemplar (archetype), given that above we explicated eminent containment of ideas in terms of such exemplars. How, then, could a mental substance cause the idea of extension? Following this pattern, it could cause this idea either by containing extension formally, which it cannot, given the nature of the mind, or by containing its exemplar. Could a finite mind contain such an exemplar? The last quotation shows that Descartes thinks an exemplar contains X formally! Now, *prima facie*, this seems to go against the whole purpose of introducing the doctrine of eminent containment. If God contains the archetype of extension as one of his ideas, God would contain extension formally, a most unwelcome result.[28] Perhaps, then, to return to a point made previously, archetypes are models outside of God which somehow contain the very property which God uses to create both physical things and ideas of them. We can only hazard a guess here – certainly by claiming that the archetype contains the property formally, the argument moves that archetype out of finite minds: such minds are not extended. As for the problem of whether an exemplar contains extension formally, those of the Platonic tradition, of which Descartes seems here to be a part, long puzzled over the issue of whether Forms exemplify the property they give to other things.

Thus, if eminent containment is to be used here as an explanation of the causation of our ideas of extension, it seems reasonable to conclude, given Descartes's ontological categories, that it is not any finite mind which eminently contains extension. Furthermore, the last quotation makes clear that the *ex nihilo* principle has a central place in the Cartesian scheme for the causation of such ideas. If we are correct, Descartes's worry in the Third Meditation that perhaps one could be the cause of one's own ideas of everything except, perhaps, the idea of God seems disingenuous. How this impacts on the Sixth Meditation proof for the existence of an actual physical world remains to be seen.

The same logic, however, creates an interesting issue with respect to God's eminent containment of extension. Even if God creates the exemplar for extension, the issue of its relation to him is murky. Obviously, the formal reality of extension cannot be a mode of God and, if it is one of God's ideas, and thus has only objective reality, one wonders how it fits into the scheme articulated in the quotation just discussed from the Third Meditation. For there, the exemplars are claimed to have the formal reality of the ideas that they cause in finite minds. It would seem, then, on this reading of Descartes's view in the Third Meditation, that, even if God creates exemplars *ex nihilo*, they are not modes of him. But however one reads the relationship between God and exemplars, and even if God creates them *ex nihilo*, there is no indication that our ideas could be created this way.[29]

Many times in the *Meditations*, and in previous works, for example, the *Optics*, Descartes claims that, at least to appearances, effects may be unlike their causes. His discussion of the generation of colours is one prime example.[30] Thus, Descartes seems to be entertaining the possibility of Humean causality, not only in the physical world itself, but especially with respect to the relation between that world and ideas. When he sees, as he writes the *Meditations*, that this threatens a total scepticism, he baulks. The invocation of the *ex nihilo* principle as a foundational truth is his way out. One may thus see the introduction of it and the attendant distinction between objective and formal reality as an *ad hoc* way of saving his system from scepticism, or an ingenious adaptation of an old principle of causality to a new situation. We think that the 'ingenious' label is much more fitting, for the reason that, with this adaptation, an entirely new theory of mind is introduced into metaphysics. Intentional entities, that is, ideas, having a wholly different logical structure from physical properties, call for a different sort of substance in which they inhere. *The distinction between mind and body is not, in our view, the imposition of a rather mysterious distinction into metaphysics, but a logical outgrowth of the necessity for solving a new philosophical problem.*

Thus, for all ideas,[31] the *ex nihilo* principle together with the distinction between formal and objective reality guarantees the existence of something beyond Descartes's circle of ideas. The guarantee was not self-evident and had to be demonstrated. A part of the purpose of the *Meditations* was to provide that demonstration. But what exactly does the guarantee secure? The answer to this question may not be so satisfying. Either there is an external, material world or there is only the exemplar for one. The latter possibility is secured by Descartes's appeal to eminent containment. The situation is closely reminiscent of Leibniz's God of the *Discourse* and the correspondence with Arnauld. Leibniz's God and Descartes's are faced before Creation with the atoms of all possible objects. Out of these, God constructs the possible worlds. These possible worlds include all possible combinations of these atoms as well as the various physics which, at least from the inside of such a world, would appear to glue these atoms and their constructs together. In some of these possible worlds, there will even be coloured objects. Our world is one in which colours are not instantiated, even though colour perceptions abound. But the *ex nihilo* principle is secure. Our ideas of sense, whether of primary or secondary qualities, have reached out – not, perhaps, to an actually verifiable material world, but at least to the exemplars from which it was created.

4

Is Hume the Cartesian Evil Demon?

The third evil demon, were one possible, could not create our ideas *ex nihilo*. In that sense, the demon could not pose a threat to a reasonable semantics for ideas. We can be sure that entities – exemplars – exist beyond our ideas and ourselves. In this sense Descartes has escaped the circle of his own ideas. But this is only the beginning of the story, important as it may be as a presupposition for the rest. Descartes, after all, wants to make his way back to the existence of a physical world, and to some knowledge about its operations. As we mentioned earlier, what stands in his way are two other demons which, we shall argue, structurally present problems similar to those posed by the demon already exorcised. Our purpose in this chapter is to decide whether or not these other demons go the way of the first.

Descartes's theory of meaning, as we mentioned previously, is reminiscent of Frege's and, although his motivation might be different, we think it instructive to compare Descartes's view with Russell's. Russell, like Descartes, had a doctrine of simples, but he had a reference theory of meaning; for him, there were no problems about the exemplification of simple properties, but only a question as to how a sentence which falsely reported a combination of simples still had meaning. Russell, of course, was trying to avoid what he considered to be the strange Fregean view that the meanings of terms were somehow different sorts of entities from that with which we are presented in sense experience.

Descartes cannot share Russell's view precisely because of the threat of what we above called the 'second demon.' This demon seems to present the possibility that there is no physical world, hence no exemplification of any property presented by simple ideas. This is the spectre Descartes (perhaps inadvertently) raises with his view about material falsity. As we have argued, for such a demon to make sense, ideas must be intrinsically meaningful, and their meanings must be provided by exemplars outside the mind which knows those meanings. This is consonant with the logic of those who feel that meaning must somehow be ontologically provided by entities that are not identical with those entities that possess meaning; meaning is a *relation* between two *kinds* of entity. The ground of the meaningfulness of a simple idea, if it is not in the physical world, must be in an exemplar. Without such meaning, the demon who might fool us about the existence of the physical world could not do his work. We would not understand what we are being fooled *about*.

In our discussion of exemplars and the 'third evil demon' hypothesis, we have spoken as if all ideas are on a par: all have meaning, so all require exemplars. Things are not so simple, of course. Descartes sharply distinguishes, we know, simple from complex ideas, and innate ideas from ideas of sense. We shall show now how sense ideas are to be related to innate ideas, so that the latter provide, *via* their relation to exemplars, meanings for both our reports of our sensations and the judgments we base upon them. Complex ideas will get meaning as a function of the simples they 'contain.' But, crucially, one ingredient will be found missing. When a person judges, say, a cube to be on a sphere, she is speaking about an *individual* cube and an *individual* sphere. The semantics of innate ideas does not in itself provide a semantics for our ideas of individuals. Seeing how Descartes handles this situation will enable us to show how he exorcises the second demon discussed in chapter 3. That demon threatens to deceive us about all the judgments we make about a physical world by somehow making us believe there is such a world when there is merely a world of exemplars.

To which ideas does the *ex nihilo* principle, as construed in chapter 3, about the meaning of our ideas, apply? It seems clear from the *Meditations* that innate ideas have the sort of semantics we have developed in chapter 3; the proof for the existence of God is paradigmatic of such semantics, since our ideas of God's qualities are certainly innate. But this hardly leaves things in a satisfactory state. Danto's original point had to do with ideas of sense, or perceptual states, and unless we can explain the relevance of innate ideas to those states, we have not addressed the issue as he sees it. Furthermore, we must explain how, at least in the *Meditations*, Descartes distinguishes between colour ideas and other so-called ideas of secondary qualities, which are not innate, and those qualities whose ideas are innate. As we shall see, his change of mind about this distinction in his later 'Comments on a Certain Broadsheet' marks a significant corroboration of our view of his semantics.

Let us begin to address this issue by an analogy. Russell distinguished between the apparent and real logical form of a sentence. It is not that the apparent form is not a form; there would not be a sentence unless it were. Yet the real form reveals something that the apparent does not. In the case of 'The present king of France is bald,' Russell argued that neither its truth conditions nor its referring terms were as they appeared to be. We, in turn, want to distinguish between the apparent and real semantical form of a Cartesian idea. Danto has worked with the apparent form; every idea of sense does seem to represent, just as the apparent form of the 'The present king of France is bald' appears subject–predicate. But analysis of ideas yields elements not apparently there in the same way that analysis of Russell's example yields quantifiers, an identity sign, and so on.

Let us start with a favourable case, as it were. Mary sees a sphere resting on a cube in her room. There is, as we ordinarily think of it, a causal connection among the cube, the sphere, and Mary's perceptual idea of the situation. There is much evidence that Descartes thinks that the shapes of bodies are not as we experience them by sense; for example, we see a tower as having a different shape than it does. Mary's visual field is characterized by perspectival geometry. Not only is the shape in our visual field not necessarily the shape of the physical object, but even Descartes's belief concerning the dimensionality of the visual field is not clear. With respect to the latter, there are two possibilities: (1) that he means we see a shape three-dimensionally, but judge it to be some other shape, also of course three-dimensionally, or (2) we *see* *two*-dimensionally but judge *three*-dimensionally. In the *Optics*, Descartes speaks as if our seeing distance out from us is judgmental, though usually unconsciously so, and he makes comparisons to how an engraver represents shapes of objects, using a flat surface.[1] But there are passages in early works where he talks in the same breath of seeing distance and colours.[2] We shall take the view in the *Optics* as the view of the *Meditations*, since he often cites the *Optics* in the latter work.

Descartes's view of the situation can now be explained in light of the revealing passage from 'Comments on a Certain Broadsheet' with which we began chapter 2. There, he speaks of the mind representing to itself figures, and even colours, on the basis of innate ideas excited by corporeal motions in the brain. So, in his view, there is a law that, on the occasion of a certain sort of brain state caused by the sphere being on the cube, a selection of innate ideas is made – namely, the ideas for the shapes as they will occur in the visual field – and there is a construction of the 'visual field' percept from this selection.[3] Thus the 'visual field' shapes do not arise *ex nihilo* from the brain state. One major point of having innate ideas is that they provide us with the material for constructing our sense fields.[4] Then, via the connection between innate ideas and exemplars, the meanings of our sense fields, or the awareness of the given itself, is also provided. Of course, Mary has learned that she cannot take her visual field *just* as given; she makes judgments that do not merely describe the given. We learn how to 'read' our sense fields; the judgment takes a crucial part of its truth conditions from other innate ideas, that is, ideas that are not necessarily identical to those used in constructing the sense field. Mary judges on the basis of her visual field (not necessarily consciously) that she is in the presence of *a* sphere on *a* cube. This judgment is made using what Descartes calls a 'natural' or 'innate' geometry.[5] As Nancy Maull puts it:

For in his explanation of distance perception, Descartes invoked the use of a *natural geometry*, innate in the percipient. This natural geometry, he claimed, processes the data of sensation so as to produce a judgment about natural spatial relationships.[6]

Upon reflection, we even find ourselves in possession of rules (actually the rules of perspective) for the projection of 3-dimensional figures onto a 2-dimensional plane. We need only 'reverse' these rules to apply a natural geometry and to form perceptual judgments about 3-dimensional objects.[7]

Our view of Cartesian semantics depends on a strong interpretation of the doctrine of innate ideas: that they are not, as R.M. Adams puts it, constitutive of

a general faculty of receiving sensible forms from sensible objects – a faculty that could be compared with the famous blank tablet on which nothing has yet been written, ready to receive whatever forms the sensible objects may impart to it. For according to Descartes, no forms come to the mind from sensible objects. The mind must innately have, not a faculty of receiving sensible forms in general, but specific predispositions to form, on appropriate stimulation, all the ideas of sensible qualities which it is capable of having.[8]

Descartes puts the matter rather revealingly, as follows:

When he [Regius] says that the mind has no need of ideas, or notions, or axioms which are innate, while admitting that the mind has the power of thinking (presumably natural or innate), he is plainly saying the same thing as I, though verbally denying it. I have never written or taken the view that the mind requires innate ideas which are something distinct from its own faculty of thinking. I did, however, observe that there were certain thoughts within me which neither came to me from external objects nor were determined by my will, but which came solely from the power from thinking within me; so I applied the term 'innate' to the ideas or notions which are the forms of these thoughts in order to distinguish them from others, which I called 'adventitious' or 'made up.' This is the same sense as that in which we say that generosity is 'innate' in certain families, or that certain diseases such as gout or stones are innate in others: it is not so much that the babies of such families suffer from these diseases in their mother's womb, but simply that they are born with a certain 'faculty' or tendency to contract them. ('Comments on a Certain Broadsheet,' (CSM1, 303–4)

To see the ontological and semantic implications of Descartes's move, let us consider for a moment what a Humean analysis of the cause of an idea of, say, red would be. If there is a lawful connection only in the sense of a constant conjunction between a certain sort of brain state and an idea of red, nothing else would be necessary in the analysis of the production of the idea at a specific time except the statement of a set of initial conditions. The very fact that Descartes invokes innate ideas in the causal story of the production of ideas shows that he would not be content with a mere Humean constant conjunction. For, given the *ex nihilo* principle, the constant conjunction in question would surely violate it – there would be no discernible match in terms of objective and formal reality, or even in terms of objective reality and eminent containment of that reality, between the brain state and the mental state. Although we shall not argue the point here, we feel that the Cartesian doctrine of innate ideas is merely an adaptation of the old Aristotelian view of potentiality to the case of the causation of ideas. The Aristotelian principle, too, has been argued by Stace to be motivated by the *ex nihilo* principle.[9]

We have claimed that innate ideas are the main semantic vehicles for a Cartesian theory of meaning. Such ideas provide a non-Humean solution to the problem of how sense ideas are caused. Innate ideas cannot be interpreted as just mere processes. Innate ideas are not a knee-jerk Aristotelian afterthought but rather a crucial part of Descartes's theory. Exactly what is the correct description of such ideas? 'The potential to produce a sense idea of red under brain state conditions C' cannot be taken to designate the content of the innate idea, but merely its form; we want its content to be merely (in this case) *red*. Just as Descartes speaks in general of the formal reality of an idea of X, where 'X' shows its objective reality, so innate ideas too have a formal reality and an objective reality. We might think of the objective reality of the innate idea of X as being shown by 'X,' and the formal reality by 'the potential to produce _____ under brain state conditions C.' That is, the last phrase is not part of the content of the innate idea, but merely shows what sort of idea it is. The form is the way in which the potentiality is in the mind – as innate idea.

The theory of innate ideas, however, cannot provide a complete Cartesian semantics. We said that Mary judges that *a* sphere is on *a* cube. Our emphasis on 'a' shows that we have yet to account fully for the semantics of her judgment. After all, Mary is making a judgment about individuals, and even if innate ideas provide the semantics for the properties which she judges to be before her, they do not provide meaning for the specificity of her judgment, for what may well be her actual claim: *this* sphere is on *that* cube.

We have already established that Descartes shows in the Third Meditation that exemplars provide perceptual judgments with meaning. Without exemplars, we must contemplate a world in which something comes from nothing, our sense fields created by God from no models. The second demon is now exorcised with the same principle that exorcised the first. Exemplars are indeed necessary for the creation of a physical world, and for the meanings of our ideas. They are not, however, sufficient for the semantics of our judgments. We do know what our judgments mean, and nothing in the world of exemplars can give both 'this' and 'that' meaning.

We spoke in the last chapter of God containing extension eminently, in the sense that there is either an exemplar (or a set of them) as ideas in the mind of God or, even, independent of him. But such an exemplar, we feel, must be viewed in the same way as Malebranche's infinite intelligible extension – to speak of infinite intelligible extension is to speak of the mathematical possibilities that could be instantiated in a physical world.[10] The issue is over what constitutes an instantiation. Can there be such instantiations without there being, if we may put it this way, models for particulars?

Before trying to answer this question, we wish to explain a bit more exactly the problem we are trying to address. It is not the traditional ontological one of individuation: what set of entities accounts for the uniqueness of *this* individual? The issue, rather, is a semantic one, and independent of the analysis one might give of what a particular individual is; that is, the issue is the semantic ground for 'this' in the true sentence 'This is a cube,' spoken or believed by common sense. We argue that such semantics do take us into a physical world, whatever its ultimate ontological analysis. Indeed, our point remains the same even if there is only one physical entity. Many commentators have worried about how many individuals Descartes is committed to; thus, if material substance is identical to its essential attribute, then, presumably, there is only one material substance. If there is only one material substance, then what we think of as rocks and chairs are not in the exact ontological sense individuals, but this is not relevant to the question of the semantics of everyday judgments about individuals.[11]

Either there are models for particulars or there are not. If there are, there is a problem in distinguishing the models of particulars from particulars themselves. In the realm of exemplars, what would distinguish one particular from another? If there were exemplars for every particular that the demon could use to fool us about the existence of physical objects, the world of exemplars would be a complete shadow of the physical world. Indeed, one might wonder what the difference could amount to, a difference without ontological bite.[12]

If there are not models for particulars, then the physical world with all its instantiations of properties is necessary for the semantics of individual judgments. How this world comes into existence is not relevant to the semantic issue. Even if there is no creation, and the physical world in all its particularity has always existed, that world is necessary for us to make the judgments about it that we do. If particulars are created, for example, by God instantiating property exemplars, say, the exemplar for sphere, then before the Creation there could be no judgments about the physical world. That is, no God or evil demon could create in us judgments which seemed to be about a physical world but which were in fact about nothing.

The above is a reconstruction of Descartes's proof in the Sixth Meditation for the existence of a physical world. Where does our idea that there is such a world come from? The structural lines of the proof, as he presents it, are familiar, similar to those invoked for the proof of God's existence in the Third. In the Sixth, he eliminates God and himself as the cause, leaving only the physical world itself. Descartes eliminates God on the grounds that God is not a deceiver; our secular construction is that God either would have to create the idea of such a world in us from a model or he would not. If the former, then the difference between that model and the physical world itself would be ontologically without force. If not, could God create an idea of an individual thing in us without its content going beyond the idea itself? No, because the idea presents itself as of something beyond itself, not just with respect to sphericity, but with respect to the fact that there is something that is spherical. That content must have a source; there is no other way to explain how contents are *individuated*, in the sense of being presented as individuals.

Could *we* be the source of our idea of the physical world? If Wilson is right, and we believe she is, that all ideas present themselves as about something beyond themselves, Mary's judgment that a sphere is on a cube presents her with an idea whose content goes beyond the idea itself. To have one such idea about the material world is to believe, at least, that there exist entities other than our own ideas. Even the *cogito* fits this model. There has been tremendous controversy in the literature over whether the *cogito* is an inference and, if it is, how one is justified in inferring the existence of one's own individual self from the fact that there is thinking. Descartes's insistence on presenting the judgment in the form 'I think' is, in our view, a reflection of his claim that such judgments are individualized; even if he is not justified in presenting the judgment using 'I,' he might have said 'there is *a* thinking'; the thought presents itself as particularized. In that sense, 'there is a thinking' is no different from 'there is a sphere.' In both cases, we must provide the semantics not only for the qualities involved (thinking and sphericity), but for the individuality expressed in the judgments. In that sense, even the *cogito* follows the general pattern of semantics we have outlined above.[13]

But if the *cogito* somehow gives us an idea of individuality – namely, from the individual who thinks – could that idea be the source of our idea of individuality which we then extend to the physical world? One must envision here something like imagination putting together the idea derived from the idea of self, together with an idea of a physical property, to produce the judgment 'this is a sphere.' An answer we believe consistent with Descartes's whole approach is this: the idea of one's own self is not of the right *nature* to combine with an idea of a physical property to produce 'this is a sphere.' Descartes makes this distinction clear in the Second and Sixth Meditations: the natures of the physical and mental preclude their combination in the sense that nothing mental can be predicated of anything physical, and conversely nothing physical can be predicated of anything mental. The upshot is that our idea that there is a physical world, given that substances have natures, cannot be derived from our idea of the self.[14]

We have thus arrived at the semantics for 'this' in the expression of the sense idea that this is a cube by a process of elimination. But such a characterization does not go very far in explaining exactly what the content of an idea of an individual is, if it is not to be construed in terms of a reflection of the semantics for exemplars. Certainly, to be consistent with the rest of the semantic scheme we have developed, there must be a law that correlates brain states as described by Descartes with, not only the shapes and colours in sense fields, but their instantiation as well – assuming that Descartes might distinguish them. Even granting this, describing the content of the idea of a particular thing without resorting to properties (*via* exemplars) is not exactly an easy task and, indeed, it has plagued philosophers from Aristotle to the present. The problem is not in recognizing that there is an individual before one's eyes but – at least from the philosopher's point of view – in characterizing what it is that we are recognizing, that is, what entity or entities constitute that individuality.

Of course if one treated Cartesian sense fields as presenting sense data, one might take the Goodman line that there are places and times, say, in the visual field, which are in effect universals and which individuate.[15] But (a) even if one grants that Cartesian sense fields present sense data, which we have argued they do not, it is not at all clear that Descartes thinks that space–time coordinates in the phenomenal field are our way of knowing individuals; (b) even if these coordinates are the way in which we know that we are in the presence of an individual, nothing follows about the ontological analysis of individuals in the physical world; and (c), to emphasize one of our points in (a), our belief is that Descartes retains a version of the notion of the substratum that Locke exposes forcefully in Chapter XXIII, Book II, of the *Essay*. The clearest evidence for this is provided by the wax example of the Second Meditation. Descartes tells us that, after subjecting a piece of wax to heat, all the specific properties of the wax change, and yet we are somehow aware of the same individual wax. He says,

but even as I speak, I put the wax by the fire, and look: the residual taste is eliminated, the smell goes away, the colour changes, the shape is lost, the size increases; it becomes liquid and hot; you can hardly touch it, and if you strike it, it no longer makes a sound. But does the same wax remain? It must be admitted that it does; no one denies it, no one thinks otherwise. So what was it in the wax that I understood with such distinctness? Evidently none of the features which I arrived at by means of the senses; for whatever came under taste, smell, sight, touch or hearing has now altered – yet the wax remains.[16]

We also know that the wax has the general characteristics that Descartes designates by the term 'extension.' Of course what Descartes is trying to show here is that there are things that we know that we do not know by sense *perception*, but rather by *conception*. Yet surely the sense field in some manner carries the individuality of the piece of wax, because it is the act of conceiving triggered, as it were, by the sense field that lets us know that there is indeed an extended individual present; again, it is not the specific properties of the wax that tell us this, since they all change.

'I must therefore admit that the nature of this piece of wax is in no way revealed by my imagination, but is perceived by the mind alone. (I am speaking of this particular piece of wax; the point is even clearer with regard to wax in general.)'[17] Such a view of the individuality of the wax certainly seems to reflect *some* view of a substratum.[18] Descartes might then see any reflection of this notion in properties as muddled. But he is singularly uninterested in the problem of what individuals are and how we know them. What we are arguing is a point not merely consistent with, but, we think, *implied* by his general semantic stance; we are the first to admit that it is not clearly addressed or articulated.

The 'second demon' problem, as we have just presented it, may appear to be nothing but the 'dream' problem in disguise. In our view, however, the 'dream' problem is merely a special case of the 'second demon' problem. As we introduced the latter, it is a question over whether there is a physical world. One can construe the 'dream' problem as raising this same issue – as opposed to the weaker reading which asks, at any given moment, whether we can be sure we are in contact with that world – but our point in introducing the second demon is to show that the question is more generalized. One doesn't need dreams to contemplate the ontological possibility that there is no physical world but that we mistakenly believe there is one because of some systematic error that we make. But there can be no such systematic error; given the causal principles of the Third Meditation, the only way to account for our judgments about individual physical things is to posit the existence of a physical world. There is, of course, a severe problem about how that world causes us to have the individual ideas of it. If there are no exemplars for individuals to trigger, the account we have given of the semantics for 'sphere' in 'this is a sphere' cannot be invoked to account fully for our sense fields or the individual judgments made upon them. But, in our view, the Sixth Meditation makes clear that Descartes's argument for the existence of such a world is at base a semantic one which depends not on the veracity of God, but on the necessity of the *ex nihilo* principle.[19]

So far, we have solved two 'evil demon' problems with the basic principle that the cause of an idea, for Descartes, must coincide with its content. Yet the principle also threatens semantic disaster. Let us return to the enhanced 'inverted spectrum' case mentioned at the end of chapter 1, which presents us with yet another version of a 'demon' problem (the first demon, as described above). Here, the difficulty is that, even if there is a physical world, and even if it is causing our sense experience, our behaviour – including our verbal behaviour – is inappropriate to that experience although it is perfectly appropriate to what caused that experience. If, for example, cubes cause sphere perceptions, but these perceptions, in turn, cause cube behaviour – behaviour appropriate to the presence of cubes – and spheres cause cube perceptions, but sphere behaviour, there would, according to the view we have of Cartesian semantics, be a seemingly insoluble problem. To see this clearly, generalize the cube–sphere problem in a Quinean way – many different 'worlds' might produce exactly the same behaviour.[20] We would have a generalized topsy-turvy world – not just colours and cubes, but everything we believe would be, in this sense, upside down.

Let us be clear about the place of judgment in this description of Descartes's position. Cubes, we speculate, cause sphere perceptions, that is, sense fields like what a sphere would cause under normal conditions. The 'inverted spectrum' view has us (a) believing, or judging, that there is a sphere, but (b) acting, or behaving, as if there is a cube, including saying aloud the words 'this is a cube.' Unfortunately, saying the words aloud doesn't help us spot the discrepancy, since we think that the semantics of that sentence are sphere semantics; as far as we know, these are the appropriate words. Nor is there any other way to spot the problem: if we, for example, wish on the basis of our belief to cut the sphere in half to get two hats, our behaviour will produce a new sense field consistent with our having produced two hats. Perhaps it would be helpful to compare this with a familiar case which at first seems similar: we see a round coin as elliptical but judge we are in the presence of a round object. Here, once we know the laws of perspective, we do not judge that we are in the presence of an elliptical object. An elliptical sense field produces the correct judgment. But, in the 'spectrum' case, the sense field produces the wrong judgment – wrong in the sense that there is no sphere.

The problem is systematic. Let us consider, by contrast, the weaker version of the 'dream' problem we discussed above. The 'dream' problem in its weaker version is not systematic. There, the issue is whether at any given moment we can know if we are in contact with the physical world. Descartes's answer in the Sixth Meditation is coherence: induction gives us at least probable knowledge of when we are awake or asleep, of when our judgments about the physical world are true. But in the 'inverted spectrum' case as we have generalized it, induction cannot tell us when there are really cubes or really spheres causing our ideas of sense. In the case of the dream, we know there is a problem, we know that sometimes we dream. But the first demon provides no clues even to the problem's existence.

For a Quinean in this situation, the answer to the question of whether there are spheres or cubes, given that we have sphere and cube ideas (i.e., the words 'sphere' and 'cube'), cannot be answered in an absolute way, independent of complex conventions and background assumptions. Functionalists, as we said in chapter 1, do have an answer – what we see is what we get, as it were. If cube ideas produce sphere behaviour, and it is appropriate behaviour, then cube ideas are about spheres; they are not really cube ideas after all.

For a Cartesian, the problem postulates a deviant causal connection between what exists physically and our perceptual idea, and a further deviant connection between idea and behaviour.[21] We shall turn to what we believe to be the Cartesian attitude towards these possibilities in a moment. For now, let us note that exorcism of neither the second nor the third demon saves Descartes in this situation. Even if there is a physical world and exemplars for spheres, the world from God's point of view would be a lot different from how it looked from our point of view.

To review the situation once more: in order for the systematic deception to occur, a physical thing, for example, a sphere, must cause an inappropriate idea. There would be, in such a case, no necessary connection between our idea, say, of a cube, and its efficient cause. Further, the cube idea behaves as a sphere idea normally would – it causes appropriate behaviour in a person who is in the presence of a sphere. The possibility of such inappropriateness is in fact a hallmark of Humean causality. In Hume's view, there is no necessary connection between cause and effect in the sense that anything can cause anything – the 'generalized spectrum' case is a perfectly successful Humean world.

That is, lawful connections do not need to exhibit any pattern upon which we could, knowing an effect, know what its cause must be. Given that Descartes clearly believes that we can and do make perceptual errors – both the contents presented by our visual field and the judgments we make on their basis can be false – it appears that he does not apply the *ex nihilo* principle to the cause of our sense ideas.

The situation is indeed Humean. We, as perceivers, are relevant variables in the production of our own ideas, yet our part in the causal process is not clearly reflected in the semantics of our sense fields. We may not know when we have jaundice, when we are 'misperceiving,' and so on. Thus neither what is presented by our sense fields nor the judgments we make upon them are *guaranteed* to be true.[22] The very possibility of error, then, seems to open the door to the 'inverted spectrum' case. The only guarantee that we could forge against this possibility is too strong: to invoke the *ex nihilo* principle here, so that there would be a necessary connection between content and the physical world, would land us in Danto's difficulties immediately. The *ex nihilo* principle accounts only for meaning, not for truth. Descartes's claim in the Sixth Meditation that God is no deceiver, then, goes beyond a guarantee that there is a physical world. Since he believes that coherence – induction – can give us probable knowledge of the truth of individual judgments, he must believe, at least implicitly, that the 'inverted spectrum' case is not a possibility. God's guarantee includes in its scope that some of our inductions work – inductions that would not help us if the 'inverted spectrum' case were real.

In his 1984 paper, 'Cartesian Error and the Objectivity of Perception,' Tyler Burge, we believe, interprets Descartes's semantic view in a way very close to our own and, as we shall show below, he implicitly invokes a version of the 'inverted spectrum' problem against Cartesian semantics.[23] We say 'we believe' because Burge's discussion of Cartesian semantics is extremely succinct, and he makes none of the distinctions between types of sceptical situations that we do. However, it is instructive to examine Burge's view in order to see more clearly what the 'inverted spectrum' possibility involves. In discussing the seventeenth-century view that the relation between an idea and what it is about is similarity, he says:

Descartes and his rationalist successors either rejected or laid little weight on explanations in terms of similarity. But they tended to retain the view that perceptual representational types carry information or have their representational characters in complete independence of the way the empirical world is. Theological and idealist considerations were imported to shore up the objective and cognitive value of perceptual representation. And the whole tradition fell prey to Humean scepticism.[24]

By 'theological considerations,' we interpret Burge to mean the appeal to the claim that God is not a deceiver. Leaving that aside, the idealist considerations are, we think, what we have termed the 'semantics of exemplars.' The problem, Burge tells us, is that such a semantics leaves room for Humean scepticism. What might this mean on our scheme which divides the sceptical possibilities into three distinct categories? The third demon is ruled out, as we saw, since with exemplars the demon cannot come between an idea and its meaning; in invoking the idealistic, Burge sees this too. Given our view about overcoming the second demon, Descartes's semantics invoke more than exemplars – there must be a physical world to ground our perception of individuals. It is not clear that Burge sees that. The following paragraph – which comes immediately after the one quoted above – seems to contrast the Cartesian semantics of the ideal with a semantics grounded in the physical world, as if Descartes's semantics are totally detached from that world.

In retrospect, this set of ideas seems strange. Not only do our perceptual presentations or experiences have the qualitative features that they have because of the law-governed ways that our sense organs and neural system interact with the physical environment. But their giving empirical information to conscious beings about the environment – their representing it – depends on their qualitative features being regularly and systematically related to objective features of the environment. No matter what their phenomenological character, perceptual presentations can represent objective empirical features beyond themselves as such only through having instances stand in regular causal relations to instances of those objective features.[25]

It is the first demon, the enhanced 'inverted spectrum' case, that presents Descartes with his greatest problem. We must take care to distinguish the possibility of there being no world at all and that of there being a world different from what we believe it to be: in the latter case there is a world, but it might not contain *any* of the properties we believe it does, given a Cartesian semantic scheme. Such a possibility is a mere variant of the enhanced 'inverted spectrum' case described above. Even if none of the properties one perceives is actually instantiated in the physical world, there still has to be, even on a Cartesian scheme, a systematic isomorphism between what there really is and what we think there is or we could not, as we do, survive – indeed, this condition seems built into the very terms of the 'inverted spectrum' problem. Seen in this light, the disagreement between Burge and Descartes comes into sharper focus. Burge believes that to overcome the first demon the semantics of perceptual ideas must be tied to the physical world and not to something beyond that world, as exemplars would be: 'It makes no sense to attribute systematic perceptual error to a being whose perceptual representations can be explained as the results of regular interaction with a physical environment and whose discriminative activity is reasonably well adapted to that environment.'[26] But Burge admits that it is logically possible that we all suffer a mass hallucination of the kind that would in effect be an 'inverted spectrum' situation: 'But I do think that we are nearly immune from error in asserting the existence of instances of our perceptual kinds, and of other kinds that are taught by more or less immediate association with perceptually based applications. I think that (induced) mass perceptual hallucination or a total lack of regularity between an individual's experience and his or her environment are the only possible explanations for an individual's perceptual experiences *always* systematically failing to apply to the world.'[27]

Thus, the difference between Descartes's view and Burge's is that, at a crucial point, Burge does not take scepticism seriously. We take it that the error that would be made if there was an induced mass hallucination is that we would think that certain perceptual properties are exemplified when they in fact are not (note that Burge says 'nearly immune' in the quotation above). To overcome this problem, Descartes has recourse to God's goodness, while Burge invokes the laws of nature as we know them, something that, for Descartes, would beg the question at issue. All we can be sure of on a Cartesian view, without God, is that, given that we survive and there is a physical world, there is an isomorphism between what exists and what we think exists.

If we are correct, then, Descartes and most of his commentators have misplaced the significance of the 'demon' problem and the issue of circularity. The most destructive evil demon comes from the generalized 'inverted spectrum' case, and if it can arise, it can do so against even the strongest semantical system that Descartes can provide.[28] Descartes can save himself from the result that all ideas are true only by denying that the *ex nihilo* principle applies in the case of sense perception and affirming that it is God's goodness that guarantees that at least some of our judgments are true. But to invoke God is to give in to the possibility of an irrational world. A rational world must conform to the *ex nihilo* principle; if it does not, anything goes. Yet, if it does conform to such a principle, it is difficult to see how there can be any false ideas.

There is, then, a core of truth to Danto's claim that, for Descartes, all ideas are true: all would be true if Descartes invoked the *ex nihilo* principle to explain the causation by the physical world of our judgments about it. In order to allow the possibility of error, Descartes must abandon the principle when it comes to mind–body interaction. Danto is in this sense right for the wrong reasons. He does not see that the intentionality of ideas does not automatically land one in semantic disaster; he fails to appreciate the place of either the simple–complex distinction or the distinction between meaning and truth, both of which allow us to have intentional ideas without a guarantee of all ideas being true. Only the enhanced 'inverted spectrum' case gets Descartes into trouble. Thus, if Danto's point is that Descartes must abandon intrinsic intentionality to avoid the absurd consequence that all ideas must be true, we disagree. Indeed, in our view, intrinsic intentionality cannot save Descartes from the spectre of the 'inverted spectrum'; such intentionality is, in a sense, too weak rather than too strong. It guarantees only the existence of exemplars and a physical world, and not the right combinations of them. It is because of the possibility of strange combinations that the 'inverted spectrum' case arises. We wish to end our discussion of Danto – and, for now – Descartes, by showing why the former goes wrong in his analysis. But first, we wish for a moment to return to a point made in chapter 1.

As we said there, we believe that Descartes's semantic theory is compatible with a scientific psychology. We can conclude this much from the possibility of the first demon: Descartes's semantics for ideas is compatible with at least scientific behaviourism. For even if the first demon is operative, we have postulated that we could be behaving exactly as we ought to, given the causes of our ideas, and certainly nothing is changed with respect to such behaviour if the causes of our sense ideas are as they should be in a normal world. The early functionalists, of course, can solve the 'first demon' problem by refusing to acknowledge its existence. The problem, given their theory of meaning, cannot arise for them. This would not convert Descartes to functionalism, although there is no reason why he could not embrace the psychological theory that functionalism embraces. Descartes, as we have seen, invokes intrinsic meaning for reasons not related to scientific concerns.

Let us return to our case of Mary seeing a sphere on a cube. Mary, of course, could be mistaken. Had she been hallucinating, the judgment that there is a sphere on a cube in her room might be false. An error by Danto can now be seen clearly: he often identifies the percept as of a physical object, for example, of a piece of wax. That Danto is thinking of sense ideas in his discussion is clear when he says that they are like pictures. But Descartes never claims that *judgments* about sense ideas are pictures; *at best* (and of course even with this we strongly disagree), perceptual ideas, for example, the visual field, are pictures. Yet Danto uses sentences which express *judgments* to describe what the sense field *intends*. Of course, Descartes need not be committed to the view that the correct description of a *sense field* embodies a judgment about the physical world. Descartes does not say that if I see an oval shape that I somehow believe, because sense ideas have intentionality, that there is an oval object. Even worse, Danto's alleged descriptions (which we believe are judgments) of the sense fields are non-propositional in logical form, so that he loses the structure, the simple–complex distinction, which is the way out of his problem. The correct view of at least part of the semantical structure of Mary's sense field is that it is constructed from innate simples whose semantics are guaranteed by the *ex nihilo* principle. It is still an open question as to whether the judgment made on the basis of these simples is true. Mary judges she sees a sphere on a cube on the basis of her sense idea, and it is that *judgment* which provides the *surface* semantical structure to her sense idea. This is what misleads Danto. After we have made a number of judgments based on sense experiences, all of us report our sense fields by saying things like 'There is a sphere on a cube' or just 'There is a cube.' And of course these judgments, in a Cartesian semantics, do have intentionality in so far as the simples that compose them have the semantics of innate ideas. But our sense fields do not literally have the same semantics; *their* 'underlying' semantics can be uncovered only if one takes off the layers of judgment that come with experience and describes these sense experiences as a 'given' is described.

One virtue of Danto's analysis is that it creates the need for closely examining the semantics of the sense field within Cartesian metaphysics. Indeed, in our view, the seventeenth- and early eighteenth-century metaphysicians were obsessed with this problem. Berkeley is not just a typical representative of this obsession but provides a paradigm for one of its apparent solutions. We turn now to his views.

5

A New Approach to Berkeley's Ideal Reality

We see the theory of ideas, advocated by both rationalists and empiricists in the seventeenth and early eighteenth centuries, as an attempt to solve an information problem: how does the mind get perceptual information from the physical environment about, say, a tree? Descartes believed that, in order to perceive the tree, there had to exist an idea, a mental item, which represents (in our view, intends) it. This move puzzled many philosophers in the seventeenth century (and continues to do so in the twentieth), and it so exercised Berkeley that he tried to overthrow representationalism in terms of a theory that only added fever to already knitted brows.

We believe that, given the functionalist critique, new light is cast on Berkeley's idealism and the logic of the steps that lead him there. These steps have been the subject of much controversy.[1] We do not intend to present detailed criticisms of any recent interpretation. However, our argument does show the exact relationship between three of Berkeley's most important arguments supporting idealism in the *Principles* and the *Dialogues*: the 'likeness' argument, the collapse of the act–object distinction, and the rejection of matter. It is the 'likeness' argument which is the main focus of our attention. As we shall see, Berkeley's 'likeness' argument has a strong structural similarity to the reasoning which drove Descartes to intentional entities. Despite some interesting clarifications of it in the literature,[2] we feel the real structure of Berkeley's argument is best revealed using a functionalist-type critique. Once that is accomplished, the collapse of act and object, which in much of the literature is either ignored or only peripherally worked into the structure of idealism, is seen to be an almost inevitable consequence of the same problems that produce the 'likeness' argument.[3]

What we wish to do, then, is rehearse some of the intellectual motives we feel may have moved Berkeley in his attempt to establish idealism. By 'intellectual motives' we do not mean 'intellectual biography,' and we do not mean to be philosophically psychoanalysing Berkeley. What we are trying to do is suggest a logical pattern of thought that fits with a certain way of construing problems about ideas and their relation to the mind – namely, information theoretically. We think that there is enough argumentation in the Berkeley texts to lend support to such speculation. That speculation is fuelled, as we have previously indicated, by what we believe is the lack of any totally satisfactory account of his idealism in the literature, as well as the related difficulties of trying to decide which of Berkeley's arguments depend on what others. We also realize that the plausibility of our reconstruction of Berkeley could be thrown in doubt by the fact that any such reconstruction could not be totally coherent. After all, since idealism is incoherent, there must be missteps in the argument for it. What we hope, then, is that the unclarities we ourselves will call attention to in his theory of ideas are Berkeley's, not ours in reconstructing him.

In chapter 2, we elaborated a set of problems, the semantic and the syntactic, that in our interpretation of Dennett must be solved by any theory of internal representations. To repeat, the problems are:

(1) *Semantic.* Ideas need a semantics – we need to know what they stand for, and their truth conditions. But to understand their semantics we need to know the characteristics of the domain of objects, the very thing the representation is supposed to provide. Berkeley's way of putting this problem comes, as we shall show, with the use of his likeness principle.

(2) *Syntactic.* Ideas, representations, have a syntax, a set of characteristics, analogous to a language, which themselves must be grasped, or else there is no understanding. Interpreting ideas means grasping how the characteristics coordinate with what they are about. Thus we *seem* to have a repeat of the original 'information' problem.

Dennett casts the 'semantic' and 'syntactic' problems in terms of a homunculus, an intelligence, that reads representations. Metaphysically, the homunculus, which has haunted AI theory, took two forms in the seventeenth and early eighteenth centuries: the distinction between a mental substance and its modes (ideas) and the distinction between a mental act, the grasping of the information, and its object, the information itself.[4] In both cases, there are entities which are thought to be mental by their very nature: substances, acts, and, in Descartes's case, ideas. Although we shall not give the argument here, we think that this list is exhaustive. Berkeley rid himself of one homunculus, the act, only to re-encounter it at the level of mental substance. To analyse these steps is to shed light on why he is an idealist, for, as it turns out, sensible qualities – those entities with which we are directly acquainted in sense perception – are also alleged by Berkeley to be mental.

Seeing Berkeley's collapse of the act–object distinction in the *Dialogues* as a response to the 'information' problem makes sense of what is otherwise a very puzzling set of moves by focusing attention on a problem discussed in chapter 2: the so-called externality, to use Dennett's term, of the object of perception with respect to the awareness of it. We shall argue that Berkeley's move to idealism makes use of a logic similar to Descartes's, yet ends with a radically different conclusion. Descartes's ideas are intentional; Berkeley's decidedly are not. Rather than represent anything, ideas are the objects that we normally think of as represented. This is at least in part a function of the fact that Descartes and Berkeley take as their starting-points radically different perspectives. Descartes starts with the assumption that there is a world independent of sense experience describable by the laws of physics and optics, the so-called third-person point of view. Berkeley appears to make no such assumptions. Rather, he insists on describing what has come to be called a 'given' in terms of sensible qualities of which we are directly aware, the so-called first-person point of view.[5]

Berkeley's ideas are not intentional; they are neither about nor represent anything. What about them, then, is peculiarly mental? In other words, why classify sensible qualities as ideas? We hope to give a new answer to this question.

Berkeley writes the *Principles*, and then the *Dialogues*, in order to reject the sceptical consequences of philosophers' claims to representationalism and material substance.[6] His goal is to provide a metaphysics for a philosophy of perception which will be free of scepticism and consistent with common sense. In this revealing passage from the *Principles* (section 73), Berkeley makes the progression of his thinking explicit:

First ... it was thought that colour, figure, motion, and the rest of the sensible qualities or accidents, did really exist without the mind; and for this reason, it seemed needful to suppose some unthinking *substratum* or *substance* wherein they did exist, since they could not be conceived to exist by themselves. Afterwards ... men being convinced that colours, sounds, and the rest of the sensible secondary qualities had no existence without the mind, they stripped this *substratum* or material substance of those qualities, leaving only the primary ones, figure, motion, and such like, which they still conceived to exist without the mind, and consequently to stand in need of a material support. But it having been shewn, that none, even of these, can possibly exist otherwise than in a spirit or mind which perceives them, it follows that we have no longer any reason to suppose the being of *matter*. Nay, that it is utterly impossible there should be any such thing ...[7]

We believe that Berkeley's intellectual motives for idealism conform to the pattern summarized in these passages. Thus, we believe Berkeley's idealism to be a consequence of a series of steps, each with independent purpose, which begins with an attack on the doctrine of representationalism. We will show that, while Berkeley is not himself in the grip of representationalism, he is convinced that sensible qualities are mental, ideas, by arguments closely related to ones his enemies use to escape problems (1) and (2) above. Berkeley is aware that in presenting such ideas to be characteristically non-intentional – since they do not in any classical way represent – he has placed his theory of ideas outside the range of traditional accounts of the mental. We shall show that the problems pointed out by Dennett then lead Berkeley to idealism; these problems force the collapse of act and object, and in so far as the distinction between act and object is collapsed in the direction of the act, he thinks sensible qualities must be mental.[8] The final step in Berkeley's procedure, as stated above, is to use the rejection of representationalism and the newly established ontological status of sensations to repudiate the doctrine of material substance.

Our view avoids the main problems of the 'inherence account' and its difficulties with section 49 of the *Principles*.[9] It does not accord with the order in which Berkeley presents his argument in the *Dialogues*. There it may appear that the argument is as follows: he argues first that sensible qualities are mental, using perceptual relativity arguments, then attacks direct realism by arguing against the act–object distinction, then finally, attacks representationalism using the 'likeness' argument. In this view, Berkeley arrives at idealism by eliminating all other possibilities for the existence of independent entities once perceptual relativity establishes the mind-dependence of sensible qualities.

But why, if one has already established the mind-dependence of sensible qualities, is the act–object controversy relevant at all? Berkeley must see that, even if one accepts the 'perceptual relativity' arguments, one might claim, as Hylas does, that given an act–object distinction, one need not move to idealism. Thus the act–object controversy stands independently of 'perceptual relativity' arguments, and the motivation for rejecting the distinction must be examined. Our interpretation of Berkeley, we think, gives him a much stronger and more interesting argument for idealism than the bad arguments – which he himself eschews in section 15 of the *Principles* – using perceptual relativity. In fact, though we shall not argue it here, we think that a strong case can be made that the 'perceptual relativity' arguments are, from Berkeley's point of view, set primarily against the primary–secondary quality distinction and not to establish the mind-dependence of sensible qualities (thus rendering the *Dialogues* arguments consistent with section 15).[10] But as we shall argue in chapter 7, Berkeley unwittingly uses 'perceptual variation' arguments to establish that it is sensible qualities and not physical objects that are directly perceived, that is, to establish the empiricist point of departure. All Berkeley needs to do in order to mount his attack on representationalism is to grant, for the sake of the argument, his opponents' belief in the mind-dependency of sensible qualities, no matter how established. Our view presents a marriage of the *Principles* and the *Dialogues* that fits pieces from both works into their logical place.

Much of Berkeley's program centres around his concept of a *sensible quality*. What is presented to the mind during a sensation or a perception are sensible qualities: we experience red, round, C-sharp, and the like. Here, as Philonous, Berkeley attempts to tell Hylas about sensible qualities:

HYLAS: To prevent any more questions of this kind, I tell you once for all, that by *sensible things* I mean those only which are perceived by sense, and that in truth the senses perceive nothing which they do not perceive immediately: for they make no inferences. The deducing therefore of causes or occasions from effects and appearances, which alone are perceived by sense, entirely relates to reason.

PHILONOUS: This point then is agreed between us, that *sensible things are those only which are immediately perceived by sense*. You will farther inform me, whether we immediately perceive by sight any thing besides light, and colours, and figures: or by hearing, any thing but sounds: by the palate, any thing beside tastes: by the smell, beside odours: or by the touch, more than tangible qualities.

HYLAS: We do not.

PHILONOUS: It seems, therefore, that if you take away all sensible qualities, there remains nothing sensible.

HYLAS: I grant it.[11]

In its next-to-last step, Berkeley's argument against the existence of material substance requires that we accept two propositions: (i) all sensible qualities are mind-dependent in the specific sense that they inhere in minds; and (ii) there are no qualities of ordinary objects or events in addition to sensible qualities. Our discussion here is concerned primarily with the attack on representationalism, from which (ii) follows. Berkeley defends this proposition in the following passages from the *Dialogues*, where Hylas lays out the representationalist model (there is an equivalent set of passages in the *Principles* – section 8).

HYLAS: To speak the truth, Philonous, I think there are two kinds of objects, the one perceived immediately, which are likewise called *ideas*; the other are real things or external objects perceived by the mediation of ideas, which are their images and representations.[12]

Berkeley attacks this model directly:

PHILONOUS: But how can that which is sensible be like that which is insensible? Can a real thing in itself *invisible* be like a *colour*; or a real thing which is not *audible*, be like a *sound*? In a word, can any thing be like a sensation or idea, but another sensation or idea? ...
HYLAS: Upon inquiry, I find it is impossible for me to conceive or understand how any thing but an idea can be like an idea.[13]

Representationalists believe that, in addition to sensible qualities, there exist qualities which are neither perceived nor perceivable. They believe also that these qualities, at least in part, are causally responsible for the perception of sensible qualities and are represented by them. It is the sensible quality pressed into the role of intermediary which becomes the focus of Berkeley's attack.

The argument is in the form of a *reductio*. Suppose that sensible qualities are *not like* the material qualities they are said to represent. In this case, Berkeley tells us, in addition to being unperceivable, the material world would be unknowable. As we would have no means by which to discover what these entities are in themselves, any claim to their existence would be empty of content. Suppose sensible qualities are *like* the material qualities they are said to represent. Since we are directly aware of sensible qualities – that is, we are aware of them without intermediaries – the same would be true of what is allegedly represented by sensible qualities. But the whole point of the representationalist argument is that there must be intermediaries. To put the point another way, if sensible qualities are like qualities that need intermediaries, we could not perceive them directly – but we do.

To elaborate: we will begin with the assumption of likeness between ideas and what they allegedly represent. Intermediaries, Berkeley argues, cannot be *like* the qualities they are presumed to represent. Berkeley is totally unrelenting on this point, as is clear from section 8 of the *Principles*: '... I appeal to anyone whether it be sense, to assert a colour is like something which is invisible; hard or soft, like something which is intangible ...'[14] According to representationalists, any effort to perceive material qualities will result in the intervention of that perception by a mediating object of perception – namely, sensible qualities. Material qualities are in that respect inherently unperceivable. If sensible qualities were like them, they too would need intermediaries to be perceived; but they are, everyone agrees, perceived directly. Sensible qualities are inherently perceivable in just the way in which material qualities are not. It is for Berkeley an absurdity to think a visual quality to be like one not visual, or a tangible quality like one intangible.

Let us turn now to the hypothesis that sensible qualities are unlike the qualities of physical bodies. Berkeley's argument here is clearly a version of the semantic problem discussed above. Sensible qualities are the alleged representatives of the qualities of physical objects. If they are unlike what they allegedly represent, then, given that we cannot know physical objects without representatives, there is no hope for constructing a reasonable semantics.

Berkeley's rather succinct argument is part of a long dialectical tradition; there is much more packed into it than it appears. When Philonous says that real things, in the representationalist view, are invisible, he means that they can be known *only* via intermediaries. In effect, he takes for the sake of the argument the representationalist view, based on the new science, that there must be a complex causal chain that links sensible qualities with the spatially external object.[15] As we argued in chapter 2, it is indeed the Cartesians who claim that sensible qualities, even sensed shapes, are not like what they supposedly represent; that the new science shows that the older view of something shared between the object and the perceptual state is naïve. Descartes, we saw, turns vice into virtue here; he uses the fact that intermediaries are unlike what they represent as the basis for a doctrine of intentionality and the corresponding new notion of the mental. Berkeley, in other words, need not be construed as begging the question by assuming that idealism has already been established, and then using idealism to attack representationalism. The difference in kind between sensible qualities and what they allegedly represent is a fundamental tenet of Berkeley's *opponents*. It is this very premise that he exploits in the 'likeness' argument.

However, it is also clear that Berkeley does not allow the Cartesian notion of intentionality; unlikeness of idea to thing represented means automatic semantic failure. In this, Berkeley places himself in a long line of seventeenth-century criticism against the doctrine of the unlikeness of sensible qualities and physical qualities. That criticism insists that representation makes sense only if there *is* likeness between the representing entity and what it represents.[16]

In summary: Berkeley would see his argument as having direct application to the model of representationalism held by an idea theorist such as Descartes or Locke. When Descartes puts sensed material qualities in the mind, the qualities cease to have formal reality as material qualities. But then, Berkeley reminds us, sensible qualities, which in Descartes's account now have formal reality only as ideas, are no longer like the material qualities they are purported to represent: *the idea of square, as a mental something, is not just another instance of square; it is not an instance of square at all.*

We have seen that Descartes would not feel damaged by this account of his theory. In both his 'Comments on a Certain Broadsheet' and his *Optics*, he explicitly acknowledges the failure of intermediaries to be like the qualities of the micro object they represent.[17] For Descartes it is innate ideas which fill the semantic gap and provide our judgments with the information which allows us to do science.[18] Berkeley, of course, as an empiricist armed with an empiricist meaning criterion, rejects the appeal to innate ideas and takes his argument against sensible qualities as intermediaries to stand.

To put the point in a different way, the results of the 'likeness' argument are as follows: either sensible qualities are mental – as the Cartesians think – or they are not. If they are mental, they cannot represent unlike physical things, nor can physical things be like them, or else physical things too would be perceivable, which by hypothesis they are not. Berkeley is clearly making sensible qualities an exception to Dennett's 'regress' problems, and some explanation must be given for this crucial move. We discuss this explanation in detail in upcoming paragraphs.

If sensible qualities are *not* mental, and like the qualities of physical things, then perceiving them would call for intermediaries as well, and so a regress looms. Hence, representationalism cannot work, whether we assume sensible qualities are mental, or whether we assume they are not. Thus, the 'likeness' argument shows that any qualities of ordinary objects or events must be like sensible qualities ([ii] above). But what is the ontological status of these qualities? There is no sustained argument in the *Principles* that sensible qualities are mind-dependent, for Berkeley never seriously doubts that they must be in some way mental. In this discussion we will do two things: first, present the logic by which Berkeley takes this position, and, second, show that his collapse of the distinction between act and object in the *Dialogues* is an effort to establish the specific ontological status of sensible qualities as ideas *inhering* in the mind. Below, we will follow Berkeley's use of this conclusion to repudiate the doctrine of material substance.

Berkeley is aware that, in accepting the conclusion that sensible qualities are mind-dependent, he must take care to distinguish the nature of his commitment to ideas from that of the representationalists. For, while Descartes's perceptual ideas are about something else, Berkeley's sensible qualities are not *about* at all.[19] Descartes solves the semantic problem with intermediaries, whose special character as intentional ideas warrants placing them in a different ontological category from material things. Berkeley solves the semantic problem by dissolving it. He also commits to ideas; but with his rejection of representationalism as well, these ideas have no information to carry. Thus, Berkeley must face some crucial questions. In what way are sensible qualities truly ideas? What is the relation of such an idea to the mind on which it depends?

First, it should be clear that Berkeley's 'likeness' argument generates initial support for the claim that sensible qualities must be mental. If they were material qualities of physical things, the necessity for intermediaries would arise. But intermediaries, we have seen, in Berkeley's view lead to insuperable problems. Hence, sensible qualities cannot be the qualities of physical bodies.[20] Perhaps sensible qualities don't belong to the physical world that necessitates intermediaries. But are not they, nevertheless, in a perfectly good sense, external to the perceiver even if they are immediately perceived? There is, says Hylas, the awareness, which is one thing, and the object, which is another. So why claim that sensible qualities are mental?[21] Indeed, Hylas's question is reinforced by the fact that Berkeley does not think that sensible qualities function in the way that was so much a part of the Cartesian tradition.

Berkeley's sudden and unexpected discussion of the act–object distinction in the *Dialogues* calls for some explanation (this discussion is absent from the *Principles*). Traditionally, acts of *perception* are seen as extracting information from objects; the representationalist view says this is done via intermediaries, but the 'likeness' argument eliminates intermediaries. Sensible qualities represent nothing. Does this fact eliminate the need for reading *them* for information, where 'reading' implies conveying of information from one entity to another? How, if at all, do we get usable information from the direct perception of sensible qualities unless they are, as it were, ingested by the homunculus to become a 'part' of it? Indeed, the whole notion of the externality of an entity from its 'reader' really comes to this: Dennett feels that, in order for information to be usable, it must somehow be 'in' the homunculus; yet there seems to be no way to obtain this result. It is this issue, we believe, that motivates not only Descartes's intentional ideas, but Berkeley's rejection of the distinction between act and object. Intentional ideas are constitutive of usable information in the Cartesian view, whether such ideas are properties of acts of awareness or objects of those acts. Such ideas are causally connected to others and, ultimately, to beliefs and actions based on them.

Berkeley claims that one is directly aware of sensible qualities. We thus have three elements in this situation: the homunculus, that is, Berkeley's mental substance; the sensible qualities; and the act by means of which the homunculus is aware of those qualities. Now it may appear initially that Berkeley, given this model, is not in a position for Dennett-like criticisms. Dennett claims (in the passage quoted above) that, if *representations* are extrinsic, that is, must be assigned a semantics, then the homunculus is somehow 'external' to the representation, the 'syntactic' problem mentioned earlier. That is, in order to assign something a semantics, its properties have to be grasped, thus reintroducing the original problem all over again. But Berkeley's sensible qualities, because they are not representations of anything, appear not to be subject to Dennett's problems. The appearance is deceptive. What creates Dennett's problems is not the fact that there is a representation, but merely that there is an entity that has to be read for information. Dennett's regress depends on the claim that the homunculus is *always* distinct from what it is reading, and the refusal (or failure) to recognize any sense of direct awareness which does not necessitate an interaction between awareness and its object, even if that object is in some sense mental. It is this interaction which presumably creates intermediaries.

Thus it seems Berkeley *should* have the Dennett problems. Let us see if he does.

After a sustained argument in the *Dialogues* in which Berkeley attempts to establish 'light and colours, tastes, sounds, etc. are ... all equally passions or sensations in the soul'[22] – equally, that is, with pain – Hylas introduces the distinction between the act of perceiving and what is perceived. He insists that one is directly aware of sensible qualities, but still entertains the possibility that they may be of a different ontological kind from awareness. Philonous forces Hylas now to present and repudiate the traditional view which saw *perceiving* as some sort of activity that must extract, or at least receive and interpret, information from a physical object.

Suppose, then, that Berkeley saw the traditional view as that of the existence of the perceiving act tied to the existence of entities that need intermediaries. Since sensible qualities are experienced without intermediaries, the act that is aware of them cannot be that of perceiving as traditionally conceived.[23] Sensible qualities are directly known. Direct awareness is not an *act that interprets* information for the homunculus. Since such acts *do* nothing, they essentially disappear.[24] There is no information gap between such an act and a sensible quality. Once the distinction between act and object disappears, Dennett's 'syntactic' problem also seems to disappear. For if there is no distinction, there is no gap between homunculus (the act) and its object, and thus no regress. Berkeley, in other words, believes he solves the 'syntactic' problem by collapsing act and object. This is the real meaning of Berkeley's remarks about the passivity of perception, and his assimilation of the object sensed to the sensing of it.[25]

But in which direction does the collapse occur? Why claim, given the collapse, that it is acts which disappear rather than the object of those acts? Berkeley really wants it both ways here. When he wants to reconstitute ordinary objects, the collapse is towards sensible qualities since, after all, that is what such objects are constructed from. But this would seem to start the Dennett problems all over again, since we now have the mental substance, the homunculus, in some unspecified relation to sensible qualities. Thus, we think, Berkeley's move to collapse the act–object distinction in the direction of the act recognizes that, to get around Dennett-like problems, one must not have an object that needs to be read by the homunculus. The object, *as act*, becomes 'part' of the nature of the homunculus; it inheres in mental substance. It then becomes difficult, to say the least, to understand what an apple is. The confusion is best seen in section 49 of the *Principles*, where Berkeley truly tries to have it both ways: sensible qualities are in the mind by way of being perceived by it! So, he retains sensible qualities as distinct from acts of awareness, yet tries to classify them as mental because they are tied to the mind by such awareness, that is, assimilated to acts which are in minds (we shall return to this point in the last several paragraphs of this chapter). As Freud would have it, competing intentions produce a slip.[26]

In 'The Refutation of Idealism,' Moore condemns Berkeley precisely on the grounds that he fails to preserve the proper separation between act and object. Moore is correct in his appraisal of the centrality of this claim to Berkeley's program. For having secured the status of sensible qualities as ideas and ideas as properties to the mind which holds them, Berkeley is ready to take on the existence of matter itself.

Berkeley presents the basic structure of his attack against matter in essentially the same form in both the *Principles* and the *Dialogues*. We see from section 9, for example, that his procedure follows precisely the outline appearing in section 73 which we noted earlier:

By matter therefore we are to understand an inert, senseless substance, in which extension, figure, and motion, do actually subsist. But it is evident from what we have already shewn, that extension, figure and motion are only ideas existing in the mind, and that an idea can be like nothing but another idea, and that consequently neither they nor their archetypes can exist in an unperceiving substance. Hence it is plain, that the very notion of what is called *matter* or *corporeal substance*, involves a contradiction in it.[27]

It is apparent that Berkeley thinks of the situation as follows: A principle of exemplification precludes the existence not only of unexemplified properties, but also of unpropertied substances: 'it seems no less absurd to suppose a substance without accidents, than it is to suppose accidents without a substance.'[28] It is enough then to show that there cannot be properties for material substance to exemplify in order for the conclusion to follow that there cannot be material substance.

So, we must be convinced that sensible qualities could not exist in matter. To that end, Berkeley in effect proposes the following *reductio*. Assume that sensible qualities could inhere in material substance. By the nature of material substance, as claimed by those who accept its existence, it is supposed to be possible for material things, that is, material substance and its properties, to exist independent of minds. It is, therefore, one conclusion of the adopted assumption that sensible qualities could exist independent of minds. By an earlier argument, it has been shown that sensible properties are, in Berkeley's special sense, mind-dependent. Hence, the original assumption that sensible properties could inhere in material substance is violated. There are no material substances, for there are no properties for them to exemplify.

Berkeley's arguments reveal the high price he is willing to pay to refute scepticism. Sensible qualities inhere in and depend for their existence upon minds, and there are no qualities besides sensible ones. All that exists is either mind or dependent on mind. Berkeley's arguments against representationalism and matter have ended in idealism. Yet, Berkeley does not see this as discouraging. Indeed, it provides him with his final challenge: to make idealism commensurate with common sense. While this is not our issue directly, there is a point to be made which reveals a confusion that has been on the edge of Berkeley's work from the beginning.

With all perceptions in the mind, Berkeley has totally removed objects from an external world. As we have shown, the only sense it makes to call such perceptions mental treats sensible qualities as, in effect, acts of a mental substance, something like Chisholm's seeing redly, and so on. In that sense, sensible qualities have lost their powers *as* qualities. On the other hand, unlike Descartes's ideas, they are not about anything either; lacking intentionality, Berkeley's ideas do not bring us information – they are what we normally take the information to be *about*. When Berkeley moves to reconstruct ordinary physical-object judgments to be about bundles of sensible qualities, his confusion becomes apparent. For now sensible qualities have somehow regained their original capabilities to qualify. But then in what sense are they in the mind? As perceived by it? If so, and sensible qualities are assimilated to acts, how can acts have the powers of qualities? Berkeley's ambiguous use of 'idea' thus makes ideas at once bits of information and bits of what the information is about.

In a way, Hume sees what Berkeley apparently does not. By collapsing the distinction between the act of sensory awareness and its object, Berkeley acknowledges that the act no longer has any work to do. Yet, he remains steadfastly committed to the mind. Hume applies the same logic which eliminates the act to the homunculus itself: if the mind does not gather and process information, what *does* it do? In effect, of course, when Berkeley reconstructs ordinary objects by positing causal connections between sensible qualities, he is already doing what the functionalists do later with information bits. Hume simply makes the logic explicit by recognizing that with the elimination of mental substance a new psychology is called for whereby information is manipulated by laws of nature.

But Hume, like Berkeley, fails to see that, once sensible qualities (impressions of sensation) are treated as information, they cannot also be treated as the very objects that the information is about. In trying to make impressions do both jobs, in his terms constructing minds out of the same entities from which he constructs objects, Hume also fails to solve the information problem, but not for the reasons Dennett believes.[29] Hume's problem, according to Dennett, still involves representational regress. Hume's *real* problem is that, implicitly sharing Berkeley's idealism, there is nothing for information *to represent*.

6

Hume's Use of Illicit Substances

Now as every perception is distinguishable from another, and may be consider'd as separately existent; it evidently follows, that there is no absurdity in separating any particular perception from the mind; that is, in breaking off all its relations, with that connected mass of perceptions, which constitute a thinking being.[1]

Hume is often classified as an 'atomist.' He is alleged to hold that every simple perception (impression and idea) is 'independent': to say that a simple perception P exists does not entail the existence of any other entity.[2] As the passage quoted above makes clear, part of this atomism is a neutral monism. That is, no perception is intrinsically mental, or material. Yet, he is also claimed to adhere staunchly to the theory of ideas. Indeed, Stroud devotes the entire second chapter of his book *Hume* to a discussion of Hume's adaptation of it. We shall argue that any plausible reading of Hume's theory of ideas identifies that which is directly perceived as *intrinsically mental*. This means either that every perception P *must be* in some mind, thus violating one tenet of atomism; or that perceptions themselves are intrinsically mental, thus compromising their neutrality. Can Hume escape this apparent dilemma?

The answer *seems* reasonably clear if one knows Hume. He claims that the mind is a bundle of perceptions. As a member of the bundle, a perception is mental. However, this notion of the mental is genuinely contextual; that is, no perception is, despite appearances, intrinsically mental owing to some non-relational quality it has.[3] To say the same thing differently, Hume holds merely that perceptions must, *as a matter of fact*, be 'in' minds in order to exist. Minds themselves are constituted by the perceptions that are in them and the relations – including causal ones – in which these perceptions stand. *Why* he thinks this, according to Stroud (and others), is probably similar to the reasons other members of 'the way of ideas' tradition classify the directly perceived as mental. More accurately, the following two propositions are considered to be merely contingent, that is, non-necessary truths, for Hume; one can imagine their contradictories: (1) In order to exist, a perception must be 'in' a mind, that is, some mind or other; (2) If a person S has a perception P, then P is 'in' S, in the sense that P is a member of a collection of perceptions that constitute S.[4] Thus, if a perception exists, it must, as a matter of fact, be in some mind or other, but it is *not* connected *necessarily* to any mind. Hence perceptions are mental, yet independent, that is, neither necessarily in the collections they are in fact in, nor necessarily in any collections at all.[5] Given (1) and (2), the existence of a perception entails the existence of a mind only in a contingent, not a logical, sense. As the reader shall see, this defence of Hume comes in the end to classifying him as some sort of phenomenalist who reconstructs the notions of mental and physical from a given database.[6]

We are not satisfied with this answer.[7] Indeed, we think it quite inadequate. To begin to show that, let us turn to a set of passages in the *Treatise* that set the problem we have been trying to outline. Hume himself speculates, in an infamous passage in the Appendix, that something is radically wrong with his claims about the self, that somewhere in his system there is a contradiction, and, indeed, he senses that the contradiction has something to do with his atomism.[8] We think he is right. Our thesis is as follows: the contradition Hume senses is that he both holds and disavows the claim that perceptions are mind-dependent in an intrinsic sense.[9] Thus, though a given perception is (perhaps) not necessarily in a given mind, it must be either in some mind or other in a logical sense of 'must,' or intrinsically mental in the sense of being intentional. Not only is this the only sense we can make of claiming, as Stroud does (correctly, we believe), that Hume adheres to the theory of ideas, but it makes sense of Hume's problems in the Appendix by showing the contradiction he fears: it is between acceptance of the theory of ideas and the claim that all perceptions are independent. In that Appendix passage, Hume claims, for example, that if our perceptions inhered in mental substances, 'there would be no difficulty in the case.' What he means is that the theory of the self would be obvious; but it also means that he would have to give up atomism. So Hume sees that, if there are mental substances, he cannot maintain the principles of atomism which he in fact does maintain. What Stroud does not see is that the very theory of ideas which he claims Hume embraces entails either the existence of such substances or intentional entities. But, as shall become evident as we proceed, Hume's phenomenalism, his view that we are only aware in perception of sensations of impression, eliminates the intentional as a possibility. That view, as we saw in earlier chapters, makes sense only if intentional entities are about independently existing physical objects. But Hume strenuously argues that we have no justification for belief in such objects. Our argument, therefore, will attribute to Hume an implicit belief in the existence of natured mental substance.

In short, our point is this: Stroud, and most everybody else, takes Hume in the tradition of the theory of ideas. The practitioners of that tradition before Hume have in common an adherence to a doctrine of mental substance or intentional entities. We do not believe that one can be in that tradition without that adherence. Since Hume cannot have intentional entities, he implicitly posits the existence of intrinsically mental substances.

That Hume is a Berkeleyan idealist or that he has intentional entities is certainly not obvious. Yet a few moments' reflection must at least raise the possibility. Hume is alleged by many to be in the empiricist tradition, following Locke and Berkeley. They both hold that what is before the mind when one perceives is an idea, and ideas surely seem to be mental entities. Locke metaphysically retains physical substances and is a representative realist. Berkeley, who eschews them, retains mental substances and is an idealist. Hume gets rid of mental substances. Does idealism go with them?

The answers to this and related questions are so imbedded in traditional Hume scholarship and interpretation that they are no longer even raised. Hume, it is often alleged, is a phenomenalist who *constructs* both the categories of the physical and the mental (and what is in them), from the data of direct experience.[10] This is what Berkeley ought to have done, but does not do. Had he done so, he would have seen that he need not hold that what is directly perceived must, in a logical sense of 'must,' be perceived in order to exist. Seeing this clearly, as Hume is said to do, also shows the way towards getting rid of the metaphysically unintelligible notion of substance. We note, in passing, that there is a strong implication in this traditional view which usually goes unnoticed – namely, that there is a connection between Berkeley's idealism and his view that there are mental substances; that is, that the mind is not a bundle of qualities.[11]

In order to assess these claims, we must turn for guidance to twentieth-century versions of phenomenalism, which shed considerable light on what is often considered their eighteenth-century role models. Although a lengthy discussion is of course beyond the scope of this chapter, we can discern two important, distinct strands in the more recent phenomenalistic tradition.

First, the neutral phenomenalism to which we have several times alluded is exemplified in the work of Goodman.[12] Beginning with Carnap's *Aufbau* as his inspiration, he carefully disavows what he calls the issue of epistemological priority which often occupies Carnap. What does this come to? Goodman's goal is to construct the world on the basis of a few qualities of, and relations between, individuals, that is, *qualia* – phenomenal colours, sounds, and so on.[13] He does not, he believes, use common sense as a *guide* in this undertaking, but only as a *check*.[14] For example, his constructions yield as concrete entities just those which we want them to yield; that is, what we know *presystematically* about which individuals have which qualities.[15] The constructions are done on the basis of systematic data: one is given only a list of atomic formulae stating togetherness relations between *qualia* and the logical apparatus of the constructional system. The rather astonishing formal result is the production of an isomorph of what we presystematically know to be true, for example, about the colour spots in our visual field and eventually, taking into account the relations in which these colour spots stand, the visual aspect of physical objects. So far forth, however, there are no entities which would group themselves into anything but bundles which are the systematic counterpart of what we would ordinarily think are *physical* objects. Presumably, other atomic individuals would have to be introduced which, on the basis of their relations to one another and to *qualia*, would constitute the mental. The mental and the physical group themselves according to the properties which the given individuals have and the relations in which they stand.

We wish to emphasize that Goodman's system may be described (though certainly not by him) as being constructed from the first-person viewpoint, that is, from the point of view of a person examining 'experience' without importation of knowledge of physical laws, psychology, and so on. It is this point of view which one finds Moore, for example, exploring in his attempts to describe the data before him when, commonsensically speaking, he is seeing a hand. The so-called argument from illusion – we have previously referred to it as perceptual variation, in deference to Austin's just remarks about illusion – plays a significant role in the production of this description. Indeed, as we shall argue in chapter 7, the role it actually plays is considerably more subtle than is normally supposed. Briefly: one is asked to 'describe what one sees' and is reminded, if she is tempted to say 'a penny,' that it looks oval and not, as it 'should,' circular, so that the descriptions must reflect only what she is sure of at the moment. Though Goodman would surely object to the characterization of being sure of the momentary and what it is that one is sure of, the idea that there is momentary experience and that it can be described apart from knowledge of nonmomentary entities, is explored by him and other, less careful, first-person theorists as well.

Second, the first-person point of view sharply contrasts with the third-person point of view.[16] Here, instead of a perceiver P describing her own experience, an observer O describes what P must be experiencing, given O's knowledge of physical laws, the interaction between mind and body (as scientifically described), and so on.[17] One excellent example of such a view in twentieth-century philosophy is Russell's in The Problems of Philosophy.[18] The progression of ideas here is simple and, from the point of view of metaphysics, deadly. One begins with the full knowledge of the properties of physical bodies as characterized by common sense and science, and then considers two sorts of 'evidence' concerning the state of P when P perceives: (a) the facts of the causal connection between, say, physical tree, sense organ, and brain involved in seeing the tree, and (b) the facts involved when there is perceptual variation, and so on. Both (a) and (b) are alleged to lead to the view that P does not directly see the physical world but something that stands between her and it. Russell, and many before and after him, unhesitatingly classify these items as mind-dependent (we take this point up in greater detail in chapter 7).

Hume believes that all perceptions, whether impressions or ideas, are mental. Indeed, the Treatise begins with this as assumed (impressions, he says, arise in the soul from unknown causes; see T7); the issue, as it was with respect to Berkeley as well, is whether there is any explicit argument for this assumption. Now, impressions and ideas of reflection surely are to be classified as mental if anything is. It may appear that Hume, in giving his 'perceptual variation' arguments (in the latter part of the Treatise section 'Of Skepticism with Regard to the Senses'), shows explicitly that as a matter of fact impressions of sensation also are mental. However, we shall argue that such a conclusion would not be justified. Perceptual variation does not establish by itself the mind-dependency of impressions; nor does Hume necessarily think it does. As we shall show, Hume implicitly assumes, in his earlier argument concerning the lack of justification for belief in the continued and independent existence of bodies, that impressions of sensation are mental. Here, however, the sense in which such impressions are mental is stronger than merely contextual. For Hume to import the later 'perceptual variation' arguments back into his earlier arguments about why we are unjustified in believing in the continuing and independent existence of bodies will not work; Hume has in mind, in these earlier arguments, another notion of the mental. We therefore do not believe that Hume is a neutral phenomenalist but rather embraces a second sort of phenomenalism, as we shall shortly explain.

Hume seems explicitly to provide, and he is certainly most often interpreted to accept, a solely *extrinsic* account of the mental. Thus, no entity is, in and of itself, mental but only comes to be identified as such as a result of certain external relationships into which it enters. This is a considerable departure from the practice of his predecessors.

Of those modern philosophers normally thought to be Hume's precursors, all maintain in one form or another a commitment to the *intrinsically* mental. The logic which guides their choices seems to centre around two doctrines. First, there is adherence to the doctrine of *mental substance*.[19] For those who are so committed, mental substance becomes the basis of the mind or self; it is the bearer of mental properties and the subject or possessor of thoughts and experience. Indeed (see below), one might hold that certain entities are classified as ideas precisely because they have a special connection to intrinsically mental substance. Berkeley is a well-known advocate of this ontology.[20] Interestingly, however, there is a major disagreement over the existence of mental substance in the period between Descartes and Berkeley: for there we find that Locke denies what these others accept, the existence of substance as natured. There are substances in which other entities inhere, but such substance has lost its essence. Substances which are mental are so only nominally. Substance itself is bare. In this respect it is Hume – at least as he is traditionally interpreted – and not Descartes or Berkeley, who stands closest to Locke, for Hume seems to deny categorically that there are intrinsically mental substances. If Berkeley is a throwback to rationalism for sticking with mental substance, then Locke and Hume are the modernists for going beyond it (Hume apparently is the bigger hero because he gets rid of the category altogether). Of course, it then becomes questionable as to what it means to classify entities as mental.

The heart of the second doctrine which shapes the view of the intrinsically mental is *intentionality*. Many philosophers in the 'way of ideas' tradition are representationalists. Whatever else that may mean, the following is a central claim of the doctrine: some items with which one is directly acquainted – namely some ideas – are said to be *about* objects in the physical world by virtue of *representing* them. Representation, as we have argued in chapter 2, *is asymmetrical*. Objects in the world which are represented by intentional entities do not themselves represent anything. Thus, intentionality must come to something other than 'similarity' of property, since normally, similarity is symmetric.[21]

Some historians have argued that the medievals, notably Aquinas, have a sophisticated sense of the intentional.[22] But Descartes and Aquinas have radically different notions of the ontological status of intentional entities. In Descartes's view, a duck in the physical world which one is, commonsensically speaking, said to see, is intended by its idea. However, it would be misleading to say that this awareness is only *indirectly* of the physical duck; the idea is an intermediary between the duck and the awareness, not because it itself needs interpretation, but because it *presents* the duck to the perceiver. Or, to put the point slightly differently, to see a duck is to have an idea based on, say, a visual presentation of the duck. The shape of the duck, while *formally* in the bird itself, is intended by the visual idea (through its corresponding innate idea, as we explained earlier), where the shape is thought to exist only *objectively*. Thus, though the duck has a shape, the visual idea does not, nor is the shape literally a constituent of the idea. It is because the shape can be 'in' the idea without rendering it or the mind duck-shaped that the idea and the duck are said to 'share' something. To put the point slightly differently, Descartes can hold that the relationship between an idea of a duck and the mind is the same as the relationship between a shape and a physical thing that has it. The idea, because of its *structure*, does not make the mind a duck.[23]

The departure from the medieval view is striking in its ontological implications. Aquinas had a notion of the object perceived and the 'thought' as 'sharing' a form. When one sees a duck, the form of the duck 'inexists' in the mind.[24] Here, the act of perceiving is a complex entity, one of whose components is the form *qua* inexistent in the mind. The form is what gives the act its content, thus 'directing' it to its object, the physical duck. The form is not an entity which must be interpreted for information about ducks. With that aspect of the intentional Descartes of course agrees; whether one considers Cartesian ideas as properties of acts or as somehow the objects of direct awarenesses, intentional entities for him are not intermediaries in the pejorative sense we discussed earlier; for example, they are not sense data. Intentional inexistence is Aquinas's way of accounting for how it is that the object makes itself known to us by, as it were, directing our thought towards it. But intentional inexistence also explains why the mind does not become a duck when the form is 'in' the mind. As we read Aquinas, the relation between the mind and the form is different from the relation between the form and the matter of a duck. Thus, Descartes and Aquinas have a very different ontological structure for intentional entities and their relationship to the mind. Of course, how the form in the mind provides this direction for the act is the mystery of the intentional.

For Cartesian representationalists, it is the intentionality of the intermediary ideas which allows us to 'perceive' the external world at all. In Descartes's view, then, an idea of a duck is a very peculiar duck, and the awareness directed at it a very peculiar awareness. Indeed, how Descartes's ideas represent is as mysterious as how Aquinas's thoughts are directed towards their proper objects. For, if the qualities in question are the same as or of the same ontological category as those that characterize physical bodies, one wonders how they 'obtain' the crucial intentional characteristic that prevents them from being characteristics of mental substances. If, on the other hand, these forms or qualities are *intrinsically* mental, if they have some sort of property of intentionality, then their relation to their physical 'counterparts' is so far forth unexplained.[25] As we have seen, it is how Descartes and Berkeley conceive of these problems that marks the crucial differences between their understanding of the mind. We will shortly see the same for Hume.

Let us summarize. For Descartes and other representationalists, some entities are about others; this aboutness is characteristic of some mental items and, indeed, is what 'makes' them mental. How these entities are invested with this aboutness, of course, is crucial. If one believes that mental substances somehow invest their ideas with intentionality, then the intentional does not provide a second sense of 'intrinsically mental.'[26] On the other hand, mental substances *may* be claimed to be such because by nature they have properties – namely ideas – which are about something. In that case, ideas are intrinsically mental 'by nature,' and one might wish to claim that the primary notion of the mental is not that of natured mental substance but that of the intentional entity, thereby raising the possibility of eliminating mental substance altogether.[27] Of course, for those in the substance tradition who have *both* natured substances *and* intrinsically intentional ideas, the connection between the two is, to say the least, close. Certainly, according to such a view, ideas and minds are made for each other, just as are qualities and the substances on which they depend. The two former categories have 'hooks' out for each other, just as many have argued is true for the two latter. When Descartes claims that the nature of the mind is to think, he may be saying (see below) in effect that intentional – intrinsically mental – entities, ideas, are characteristic of minds.

For Descartes, Malebranche, Berkeley, and Hume, *the objects of sensory awareness are mental.* In this respect all are in *the way of ideas* tradition.[28] However, if to be in 'the way of ideas' tradition means to accept the intrinsically mental, then Hume would officially have to deny that affiliation. We are going to show that it is on this issue that Hume makes the mistake which he senses so strongly in the Appendix but fails precisely to identify. Hume's portrait of ordinary objects and persons both excludes and depends on a commitment to intrinsically mental objects. Indeed, it is not clear to us how one could be in 'the way of ideas' tradition without such commitment.

Like Berkeley before him, Hume gives precious few arguments that directly establish that the objects of immediate awareness, that is, impressions of sensation, are mental. It is possible, of course, to attribute to Hume the arguments we have attributed to Berkeley. Ultimately, this is what we shall do. Not only did Hume read Berkeley; he *is* Berkeley. But, *prima facie,* such a conclusion ignores Hume's clear and forceful rejection of mental substance. It seems that, at the crucial juncture of Berkeley's argument, were he considering the ontological status of sensible qualities, Hume could not present a coherent characterization of the mental apart from a contextual one, and so could not make a move to the strong idealism that Berkeley embraces. After all, without mental substance or intentionality, what does the notion of the mental come to? Of course, one can try to provide, as Goodman does, a contextual sense. It certainly appears that this is what Hume *wants* to do. Yet he classifies *all* perceptions as mental. What sort of contextual notion could this possibly be? Hume's intentions thus conflict with his deepest conclusions.

We can best understand Hume's problem here if we reconstruct his move to the theory of ideas. We begin by exploring Hume's theory of the mental as it plays a role in his arguments about our belief in the independent, continued existence of physical bodies. We shall show that, in his arguments, Hume makes an assumption about the mind-dependence of perceptions that goes beyond anything he could have reasonably concluded from the arguments from perceptual variation. It is the latter argument which is often pointed to as Hume's reason for claiming that impressions of sensation are mind-dependent.

Hume's explanation of our belief in the continuing existence of unperceived bodies is notoriously elusive. Stroud, for example, despairs that it is difficult to see how Hume's elaborate discussion of the constancy and coherence of perceptions explains the origin of the idea of continuing existence, let alone our belief that there are continually existing things.[29] Yet Stroud, careful as he is, does not spot the key to the problem. It is not merely that constancy and coherence, the mainstays of Hume's four-part system, are obscure; rather, there is, we shall argue, a hidden assumption in the discussion which necessitates the construction of the system that embodies that obscurity. This hidden assumption is Hume's implicit idealism. That idealism, we shall show, fashions the entire discussion in 'Of Skepticism with Regard to the Senses,' as well as key passages in his discussion of the derivation of the idea of the self. Its main influence is on Hume's claims concerning the place of causal reasoning in forming our belief in continued existence.

Early in the *Treatise*, it does not seem as if there will be a problem in explaining belief in the continuing existence of independent, that is, unperceived, bodies:

We readily suppose an object may continue individually the same, tho' several times absent from and present to the senses; and ascribe to it an identity, notwithstanding the interruption of the perception, whenever we conclude, that if we had kept our eye or hand constantly upon it, it wou'd have convey'd an invariable and uninterrupted perception. But this conclusion beyond the impressions of our senses can be founded only on the connexion of *cause and effect*; nor can we otherwise have any security, that the object is not chang'd upon us, however much the new object may resemble that which was formerly present to the senses. Whenever we discover such a perfect resemblance, we consider, whether it be common in that species of objects; whether possibly or probably any cause cou'd operate in producing the change and resemblance; and according as we determine concerning these causes and effects, we form our judgment concerning the identity of the object.

Here then it appears, that of those three relations, which depend not upon the mere ideas, the only one, that can be trac'd beyond our senses, and informs us of existences and objects, which we do not see or feel, is *causation*. (T74)

What is Hume committing himself to here? It certainly seems to be that, if there is causal reasoning going on via the principle of association of causation in the cases he cites, it is done upon the observation of the constant conjunctions of physical objects and events. Furthermore, if we consider causation as a philosophical relation, we have here genuine constant conjunctions which would justify the belief that physical objects exist unperceived.[30] Granted that sometimes we associate causally on the basis of 'bad' constant conjunctions, there is no *prima facie* reason to think that this case is one of them. Given these implications, the knowledgeable reader of Hume must be taken somewhat aback; this does not sound like the arch-sceptic of all time talking. Yet there are no qualifying passages around the one just cited.

Hume now embarks on his long analysis of the causal relation. He then turns, in the section, 'Of Skepticism with Regard to the Senses,' to a detailed explanation of our belief in the continuing existence of unperceived bodies. He uses as one illustration a fire that one observes, after leaving one's chamber and then returning, to have changed in the interim. Since we are accustomed in other instances to seeing the fire burn down, we here reason from what he calls the 'coherence of the change to the belief' that the fire existed when we were not in the room. We have in the past observed five-log fires burn down to four-log fires and then to three-log fires. We light a five-log fire, leave the room, and return to a three-log fire. Using coherence as our guide, we reason that there was a four-log fire while we were gone.

What sort of reasoning is involved here? Surely it seems causal, just as in the case cited above from T74; indeed, Hume's choice of the term 'coherence' has a decidedly causal echo. We would ordinarily think of the cause of the four-log fire to be the burning of one of the five logs, and the cause of the three-log fire to be the burning of another of the logs. Thus, when we start with the five-log fire, we anticipate a four-log fire, even if we don't see it, and when we return to a three-log fire, we reason that it was caused by the burning of one of the four logs that existed when we left the room. This explanation seems not only consistent with, but nicely illustrative of, the above quotation. But, after giving another set of examples of coherence involving the famous case of the porter ascending his stairs to deliver a letter to him, Hume pulls out the rug:

But tho' this conclusion from the coherence of appearances may seem to be of the same nature with our reasonings concerning causes and effects; as being deriv'd from custom, and regulated by past experience; we shall find upon examination, that they are at the bottom considerably different from each other,

and that this inference arises from the understanding, and from custom in an
indirect and oblique manner. (T197)

Hume's denial of causal reasoning here is, to say the least, surprising.
As we shall show, it focuses attention on the exact nature of what he
believes causal reasoning to be.

Price discusses the question of why Hume believes that the case of
coherence does not yield to a causal analysis.[31] His argument centres on
constant conjunctions. Price notes that in his discussion of necessary
connection – and, we may add, in the quotations above about continuing existence – Hume generally uses examples of constant conjunctions
between physical objects and processes. But, of course, Hume believes
that the notion of physical objects and processes is built up from sense
impressions by means of the imagination; this is the whole point of the
discussion of continuing existence. That is, the idea of a physical object
essentially includes the idea of *continuing* and *independent* (non-perceived)
existence; the latter ideas both logically and psychologically precede the
former. So, at least to begin with, the problem seems to be that Hume's
examples are, at best, ill-conceived. Talk, as in T74, about belief that, say,
a mountain exists when we are not perceiving it, already presupposes
that we have the idea of the mountain as a physical object. But this idea
surely depends already upon the belief in unperceived entities; after all,
that's part of what we understand by 'mountain.' The upshot is that
Hume's examples need to be redescribed before we can assess the
proper place of causation in reasoning as to the existence of unperceived
entities.

Let us try to make this point clearer. Hume believes that, whether the
vulgar know it or not, what we are presented with in sense experience
are momentarily existing impressions. This would put the vulgar mind
in a philosophical frame, *if* what is implied is that the vulgar must *know*
unconsciously that sense impressions are momentary and fleeting (certainly we don't seem to know consciously in everyday life that what we
are aware of in sense perception are mind-dependent impressions). Not
that Hume is above such attributions; as Stroud documents, he often
gives the vulgar mind philosophical views. But, at several places in the
Treatise, Hume also insists that the vulgar take their perceptions as their
objects. If this is taken as it seems intended, the vulgar would take what
Hume calls impressions as already at least independent of perception,
and hence would never dream of the description of perceptions as
momentary and fleeting; indeed, this seems to be his position in the

Enquiry. In his discussion, Stroud claims that Hume 'provides no description of the state of the vulgar consciousness before the acquisition of the idea of continued and distinct existence, out of which that idea could naturally arise. What he needs is a description of the way the vulgar take things to be that attributes to them neither a belief in the continued and distinct existence of what they perceive nor the philosophical view that all they perceive are "internal and perishing existences."'[32]

Of course, it could be argued that, given Hume's theory of association as a model, it is not necessary that the characteristics of impressions be grasped in order for these characteristics to be causally efficacious. That is, if the existence of momentary impressions is the true state of things, such impressions might be the causes of our ideas of continuing and independent existence in the way that Hume describes without there being any awareness at all of the characteristics of these impressions.

But, given the view that we are presented with momentary impressions, Hume's examples of both the fire and the porter are, on his own grounds, at best quite misleading, since they invoke physical objects, which are continually existing things, as the elements upon which reasoning to the existence of non-perceived entities takes place. A more careful analysis must start with perceptions and show how the idea of continuing, unperceived existence is built or derived from them. Notice, too, that the causal connections in the first quotation from Hume above are between what we already believe to be continuing existents. The question, then, is whether we can clean up Hume's examples by using only perceptions as the building-blocks, and by so doing, perhaps resolve the discrepancy between the earlier and later view of the place of causation in the process. The issue then becomes whether or not causal reasoning plays a crucial role in the building of the idea of physical objects.

On the face of it, there are some causal connections among sense perceptions. Hume formulates laws – laws of association, the copy theory of ideas – whose *relata* are sense impressions. Such laws involve constant conjunctions. What is the correct description of the data on which such claims of constant conjunctions are based? In order to answer this question, let us turn to an example which, we think, presents some alternatives.

Suppose someone has some impressions of sensation, say, seeing some moving shapes and colours, and then hears a squeak. We assume, to put the subject in the situation we think Hume must be envisioning in his analysis of the derivation of the ideas of independent and continuing existence, that she does not yet have these ideas. Later, she will identify the shapes, colours, and squeak as those of a moving door. Now assume we have a situation in which our subject observes, say, the first members of the conjunction. Then, by the associative habit known as cause and effect, she should expect, given Humean principles, to hear a squeak. Finally, let us suppose, she actually hears the squeak. The habit has been reinforced, and this is nothing less than the belief that the moving coloured shapes cause the squeak.

Let us now suppose that for some reason the subject stops her ears, leaves the room, turns her attention elsewhere – and thus does not hear the squeak. Hume addresses this situation in detail in a passage which we think is at the heart of the *Treatise*:

For 'twill readily be allow'd, that since nothing is ever really present to the mind, besides its own perceptions, 'tis not only impossible, that any habit shou'd ever be acquir'd otherwise than by the regular succession of these perceptions, but also that any habit shou'd ever exceed that degree of regularity. Any degree, therefore, of regularity in our perceptions, can never be a foundation for us to infer a greater degree of regularity in some objects, which are not perceiv'd; since this supposes a contradiction, *viz* a habit acquir'd by what was never present to the mind. But 'tis evident, that whenever we infer the continu'd existence of the objects of sense from their coherence, and the frequency of their union, 'tis in order to bestow on the objects a greater regularity than what is observ'd in our mere perceptions. We remark a connexion betwixt two kinds of objects in their past appearance to the senses, but are not able to observe this connexion to be perfectly constant, since the turning about of our head, or the shutting of our eyes is able to break it. What then do we suppose in this case, but that these objects still continue their usual connexion, not-withstanding their apparent interruption, and that the irregular appearances are join'd by something, of which we are insensible? But as all reasoning concerning matters of fact arises only from custom, and custom can only be the effect of repeated perceptions, the extending of custom and reasoning beyond the perceptions can never be the direct and natural effect of the constant repetition and connexion, but must arise from the co-operation of some other principles. (T197–8)

Hume's conclusion is that the situation in which the person turns her head or her attention constitutes a counter-example to the habit she has hitherto formed. What is his reasoning here? It seems that, in order to take not hearing the squeak as a counter-instance to the habit, he must assume that the anticipatory belief is that a squeak will be *heard*, not merely that the squeak will exist whether heard or not. But clearly it is because we have described the situation in terms of expecting *to hear* a squeak that there could even be the problem that our expectation is frustrated. Ordinarily, we do not describe what we experience in terms of the fact that it is experienced. We say that we observe the colours and shapes, not that we observe that the colours and shapes are being observed by us. Thus, we describe the situation in question as the constant conjunction of colours and shapes, on the one hand, and squeaks on the other. Of course, speaking colloquially, we expect to hear a squeak. But in order to describe the constant conjunctions in terms of heard squeaks and seen colours and shapes, Hume must believe that the fact that the colours, shapes, and squeaks are perceived *is a relevant variable* in the content of the constant conjunction, an identifiable feature of both cause and effect. If Hume did not have this belief, then there would be no reason whatever for him to think that the squeak is going to be *heard*, only that it could be heard if one were there to hear it.

We are not questioning Hume's claim that the mind will not, in inductive reasoning, go beyond the constant conjunctions it has recorded (since we, as part of the vulgar, do end up believing in the continued existence of bodies, our route to that belief must be other than induction if he is correct). Our point is that his reason for the claim that the mind will not go beyond the *conjunctions in question* must be idealistic. This is the only reason that makes his otherwise puzzling claims about causation in the case of coherence sensible.[33] Hume is assuming that the correct description of the subject's habit is that she has conjoined perceived colours and shapes with perceived squeaks; that they are perceptions is part of what she is experiencing. The only reason for that assumption, as we shall now explain, is Hume's Berkeleyan idealism.

Let us look at Hume's problem here in a bit more detail. What does it mean, for Hume, to notice the squeak as perceived? Could we, for example, claim that Hume is invoking an act–object distinction, so that a mental act of hearing accompanies each instance of a squeak? With mental acts it would be possible to consider relations that a perceived perception might bear, or, as in Hume's case, would be lawfully compelled to bear, to the perceiv*ing*, as the cash value of the claim that perceptions are mental. This would not require that impressions be members of mental structures. But Hume denies, as does Berkeley, that there is any such distinction.[34] The collapse of the act–object distinction eliminates the possibility that perceptions may be lawfully linked with minds without being their constituents. Since Hume denies there are mental acts, a perceiving can be nothing more than a perception or a string of perceptions, parts of a mental structure (a mind). Hume's claim that the existence of a perception depends upon its being perceived requires that every perception be part of such a string and, thereby, of such a collection.

Could the squeak itself be intrinsically mental somehow? The only sense we could make of this would be Cartesian, if squeaks were intentional entities. But, as we have argued in chapter 5, intentionality of ideas makes sense only if such ideas do not, at the same time, serve as qualitative constituents of the bundles that are ordinary objects; whereas Hume wants ideas to serve *both* functions.

It may thus appear that in 'Of Skepticism with Regard to the Senses,' Hume has embarked on a gigantic question-begging operation. In attempting to account for the origin of our belief in the continued and independent existence of bodies, he shows that that belief cannot be rational because underlying any rational move we might try to make is the belief, whether or not we know we have it, that sense impressions are mind-dependent. It is crucial to see that Hume's idealism here cannot be of what we shall call the weak variety – that, as a matter of fact, sense impressions are always perceived, and in that sense mind-dependent. As we shall show in some detail, not only is there no way to establish such a claim empirically, but it also cannot fit Hume's explicit ontological picture of the mental. Rather, the idealism is of the Berkeleyan type. Sense impressions *must be* perceived in order to exist, and this sense of 'must' is logical. In order to hold this view, Hume must implicitly commit himself to natured mental substance, the very entities he argues later in the *Treatise* are ontologically illicit.

Hume may think he has established only that each perception as a matter of lawful fact must occur in some mind. In a best-case scenario for Hume, he would have an argument to show that all sense impressions are mind-dependent; this argument would not be *a priori*, but contingent. He could then use this argument to block any induction one might try to make to the existence of unperceived sense impressions; one could construct a self from these perceptions, and Hume's view would appear consistent and plausible.

What would an argument look like that concludes that, as a matter of lawful fact, perceptions must be perceived? Of course, Hume has not done experiments with other human subjects; his is armchair psychological speculation at best. But how could he establish the law, even in his own case? How could he be confident that there were no unperceived impressions? The problem is confused by the fact that he seems in 'Of Skepticism with Regard to the Senses' to be trying to prove just that by showing that the mind cannot reasonably go beyond what is perceived. But, as we have shown, his argument is question-begging, since the only reason for not being able to use causal reasoning to go beyond what is immediately perceived rests on the assumption that the mind already 'knows' the law in question.

In 'Of Skepticism with Regard to the Senses,' Hume seems to be treating the mind like a reasoning machine. He is asking whether the mind can move from a certain set of observed constant conjunctions via inductive reasoning to the existence of an unperceived impression. His answer is in the negative because he assumes in his discussion that the mind holds as a premise that impressions must be perceived to exist. So the issue now is whether Hume has some argument independent of the early argument in 'Of Skepticism with Regard to the Senses' to establish weak idealism.

Though it comes after the discussion of why we all believe in the existence of unperceived entities, one may wish to claim that the argument from perceptual variation underlies weak idealism. After all, following his discussion of coherence and constancy, Hume reminds us, via the argument from perceptual variation, of the fleeting, mind-dependent status of impressions. One might construe these arguments to show that impressions of sensation as a matter of fact are always perceived. In other words, if one imports the arguments from perceptual variation back into the discussion of coherence and constancy, one might be tempted to claim that Hume is right, after all: the correct description of the data from which causal inferences are made, whether we know it consciously or not, yields the *perception* of the impressions as a relevant variable. To put the point succinctly, 'perceptual variation' arguments underlie the assumption that any induction to the existence of independent physical objects cannot be justified.

But this cannot be the structure of Hume's view. As he presents the argument from perceptual variation, he believes that it establishes the mind-dependency of all objects of perception (T210–11). But even a cursory examination of Hume's arguments (pressing the eyeball, etc.) reveal – as we shall show in detail in chapter 7 – that the argument essentially depends upon the assumption of an independently existing physical world. He then claims that some philosophers now distinguish between appearance and reality, between mind-dependent and mind-independent objects as a result of perceptual variation. Hume reminds us that any belief in the existence of such independent objects itself depends upon the analysis he has given in 'Of Skepticism with Regard to the Senses' for why we believe in such things![35] Thus it seems that, in correct logical order, (1) the argument from perceptual variation relies upon the claim that there are independently existing things, but (2), the claim that there are independently existing things Hume believes to be unjustifiable. Moreover, as we have seen, Hume's analysis of *our belief* in independence itself stems from the strong idealistic assumption we have exposed. To claim now that this assumption is itself reliant upon a weaker argument – namely perceptual variation – is to run into a vicious circle.[36]

To further bolster our claim that Hume is in fact a strong idealist, let us turn to what the implications of weak idealism would be if Hume wishes to maintain, as he does, a bundle theory of the self. He also maintains a bundle theory of physical objects. The two bundle theory may be considered to be part and parcel with Hume's atomism. We shall argue that his atomism is incompatible with the claim that all impressions of sensation are mental; this is the contradiction, mentioned early in this chapter, that Hume senses in the Appendix. To say the same thing differently, we believe that Hume's final view uses the same preconceived notion of the mental that is operative in the argument against the induction, above, to the existence of unperceived *qualia*. Weak idealism only seems to be an option; there is no good sense in which Hume can claim that, *as a matter of fact*, all impressions of sensation are mental.

In order to demonstrate how the idealistic assumption infects Hume's entire ontology, let us compare once again his ontological scheme with that of Goodman. Goodman, we maintained earlier, is a neutral phenomenalist who constructs the mental and the physical contextually, from relations in which impressions stand. Can one do that and end up some sort of idealist? Goodman begins from the first-person point of view. No 'building block' of Goodman's system is intrinsically mental or intrinsically material. But Goodman does not end up as an idealist. Why not? Why doesn't he end like Hume, with the belief that all his atoms are mental or, perhaps we should ask, why doesn't Hume end like Goodman, where clearly not every atom is mental?

In *The Structure of Appearance*, Goodman begins his constructions with *qualia*, basically Hume's impressions of sensation. Using only a few relations and Carnap's schema, he constructs physical objects as, basically, classes of bundles of *qualia*. But Goodman begins *only* with *qualia*. That is, he does not have as part of his arsenal of atoms what Hume would call 'impressions of reflection.' How does Goodman know that these are not relevant in the construction of physical objects? Quite obviously, Goodman has one eye on the common-sense data to be explained, that is, as we have put it, one eye with a third-person point of view. Here common sense is more than a mere check; it is indeed a guide. Common-sensically we don't put impressions of reflection in the same bundles as impressions of sensation. In other words, Goodman, with a nod to common sense, already has his atoms categorially differentiated.

Perhaps, however, one need not invoke the third-person point of view. Perhaps one could, merely from the atomic statements constituting data, construct the categories of the mental and physical. Then we would have a clearly defined sense of the mental and the physical totally isomorphic to what we have in common sense. That, at least, would be the ideal. But now a Hume might object: if one looks at the data carefully, one will see that there is a relationship between impressions of sensation and reflection such that the former in some sense 'depend' on the latter. Let us look at this possibility more closely.

Suppose that Hume has contextually defined the physical and the mental as Goodman would like, so that *qualia* are members of physical bundles and not mental bundles. If *qualia* were mental in the sense alluded to, then they would be in the mental bundles. Thus, if one is going to classify them as mental – as Hume does – either one has a second sense of 'mental,' or one tries to show that, after all, *qualia* stand in the requisite relations that should have classified them as mental in the first place.

Hume believes that every member of a material bundle is also a member of a mental bundle, but not vice versa. But what sense of 'mental' must he be using in order to make such a claim? Clearly, it cannot be the sense in which he would have originally distinguished the mental bundles from the material ones. There, contingent relations among impressions of reflection and ideas would justify our putting them in one bundle, the mental, whereas other contingent connections among *qualia* would allow us to put them in what we call the physical bundle. Even if we could find a correlation between impressions of sensation and ideas, or more generally, impressions of sensation and (somehow) the mental bundle itself, why would such a correlation justify putting *qualia* into the mental bundle? We might just as well throw ideas (if these are the correlated items) into the physical bundle, or the entire mental bundle into the physical one. Thus, if Hume insists on putting impressions of sensation into the mental bundle – which he does – he must have a pre-conceived sense of 'mental' in mind that is even stronger than the one constructed from the relations among what we presystematically think of as mental items, for example, impressions of reflection and ideas. The contextual sense of 'mental' thus contrasts sharply with this other sense, which we think is based on the logic of an ontological category. That is, Hume is implicitly assuming about impressions of sensation what Berkeley says about ideas – that they are mental because they inhere in a mental substance. Even stronger, in order to get such a result, Hume must embrace the sort of argumentation that we attributed to Berkeley in chapter 5.

This conclusion, of course, sharply contrasts with Hume's stated position with regard to the analysis of the self. Hume's view of the self is that it is a bundle of perceptions, with causal connections holding between different perceptions in the bundle. But, as we have just shown, the view of the self as a bundle cannot be consistently maintained with the idealistic assumption. If the self is merely a bundle, the idealistic assumption no longer makes sense, and the door is opened to justifiable inductions to the existence of unperceived *perceptions*. Hume cannot maintain both that the self is a bundle and that the world is constructed out of mind-dependent perceptions. Thus, Hume's entire criticism of our belief in physical objects and a continuing self rests not on problems about induction, but on his refusal, because of his idealism, to allow a particular application of induction.

7

Berkeley and the Argument from Perceptual Variation

Historically, the argument from perceptual variation has played a key role in the attempt to establish idealism. At least, many believe, it is central to arriving at a theory of ideas. So far in this study, we have given perceptual variation in its usual form little attention. As we interpret Descartes, perceptual variation is merely a way of calling attention to aspects of the more generalized 'demon' problems. In chapter 5 we claimed the argument seems to Berkeley to be more germane to the breakdown of the primary-secondary quality distinction than the direct establishment of *esse est percipi*, and in chapter 6 we discussed the argument in relation to Hume's idealism. However, we shall see that a close examination of Berkeley's use of 'perceptual variation' arguments shows that, although he cannot arrive at idealism from these arguments *alone*, perceptual variation plays a significant role in the establishment of the view that it is sensible qualities that must be the starting-point of his empiricism.[1]

Galileo and Descartes attack a naïve view of perception in terms of a new and relatively sophisticated causal theory. The problems with maintaining the naïve view against it seem insurmountable. Both use the primary–secondary quality distinction to focus on what they believe to be the major consequence of the causal theory: the gulf between appearance and reality. The world is different from how it appears perceptually: we see colours, but there are no colours in the material world; we hear sounds, but there are no sounds in the real world; and so on. Galileo and Descartes cast doubt on our most fundamental beliefs about the external world and our access to it. Descartes maintains that the distinction between appearance and reality forces us into recognizing that we know the physical world only through the representation of it to us by ideas.

Berkeley, notorious for his responses to the problems raised by Galileo and Descartes, presents a theory of ideas which leads to idealism.[2] While denying the validity of the primary–secondary quality distinction which originally motivated them, he is not able to return to a straightforward, naïve view of perception. It is widely accepted that the crucial ingredient in his reasoning is the argument from perceptual variation (often called the argument from error and illusion). Indeed, many believe this argument is central to arriving at *any* theory of ideas.[3] Why one might think that one can arrive – or that Berkeley in fact does arrive – at idealism from perceptual variation is a function of the way one describes what one is aware of in perception. Berkeley begins with the claim that it is sensible qualities that are the direct objects of perception. He gives almost no direct argument for this claim. Our goal in this chapter is to expose his intellectual motives for it. Towards this end we discuss the argument from perceptual variation from a recent pair of perspectives – namely, those of Ayer and Austin – and show their relevance to Berkeley and the theory of ideas.

Here is a long-standing interpretation of Berkeley. He analyses physical objects as bundles of sensible qualities; both the bundles and the qualities are in some sense mind-dependent. The reason that physical objects are mind-dependent bundles stems from the argument from perceptual variation. That argument, it is alleged, forces one to remove all sensible qualities from the physical world and to place them in minds. But, since we all know there are trees and chairs and tables, and allowing for the constraints placed on us by Berkeley's assault on representationalism, such objects must be reconstructed from the mind-dependent sensible qualities, and that is what Berkeley does. Since the argument from perceptual variation thus appears central to Berkeley's idealism and his subsequent reconstructions of the physical world, we wish now to explore it in more detail.[4]

The argument from perceptual variation appeals to what is taken to be an undeniable fact of perception: objects sometimes do, and potentially always can, appear other than they are. That is, they appear, or through changes in the conditions of perception can be made to appear, to have properties they do not really have. This argument assumes from the outset that there are material objects, and that they have colours, shapes, and all those attributes beloved by common sense.

The argument proceeds as follows. Common sense believes objects can exemplify only one property under a given category at a given moment (one shape in the same space, one colour in the same space, etc.) and, in addition, that they can hold their properties over time, other things being equal (where there are changes they are explainable in terms of standard lawful relations). What follows from this belief and the facts of variation? To answer this question we will make use of the distinction between third- and first-person points of view.

Third- and first-person are points of view on the objects of perception. The third-person view describes the perceptual situation that either he, T, or another person, F, is in when T knows the laws of perspective, conditions of perception, and the laws that connect sense organs to entities in the physical world. Suppose T knows that a coin before him is round and is querying another person, F, about what she sees when she looks at the coin from, say, an angle of twenty-five degrees above the horizon on which the coin lies. T asks F to describe what she sees. J.L. Austin quite rightly points out that, if F is a normal adult perceiver, she will almost certainly say 'a coin,' with the implication being that the coin is, of course, round. F, in other words, is T's epistemologically identical twin.[5]

But many philosophers, for reasons we wish to explore in detail, make a set of moves here which, as Austin points out, lead to sense data, or even to idealism. In this case, F, according to T, will report that she sees something that appears oval or, even worse, that she sees something oval. Why she would do this, unless she had some genuine doubts that there was a round coin present, certainly needs to be explained. But suppose for a moment that this is F's report. T may be tempted to say that the reason F reports that she sees something that appears oval, or even that is oval, is that the something looks to her just like an oval thing would look under normal perceptual conditions. Or, to use more traditional terminology, T might say there is *no intrinsic difference* between the two perceptual experiences. So something that appears oval, but may not be oval, gives one the same perceptual experience as something that is oval. This is the key move in the argument from perceptual variation.

The temptation to make this move is partially accounted for by the fact that, given that T knows the laws of perspective, that is, how things should look from every angle, he could say that round coins appear round from angle A, oval from angle B, and so on. That is, there seems to be a use of 'appears' in which it is legitimate to describe how things are in terms of how they appear. What are the implications of this use? In the case of F reporting that she sees something that appears oval, 'appears' may well mark F's knowledge that things are *not* as they appear. In other words, F is not necessarily claiming or implying that the coin looks or appears like a really oval thing appears under the conditions in which an oval thing appears oval. If she is a mature perceiver and knows the laws of perspective, and so on, she will use 'appears' as in: 'Well ... it sort of appears oval, but I know it's round.' So this use of 'appears' is perfectly harmless; it only describes how the coin should look from any given perspective, given the laws of nature and the way perceivers are built. Austin can sanction this use of 'appears' in philosophical discussion because no conclusions can be drawn from it of any ontological import.[6] Coins should look round from certain angles and should look oval from others.

The sanction has its limits. Austin would surely reject the claim that the coin appearing oval to F is not perceptually or 'intrinsically' different from something that really *is* oval; really oval coins appear oval under certain conditions, and really round coins appear oval under certain conditions, and it is precisely the difference in such conditions that T is ignoring.[7] To say that a round coin appears oval from a certain perspective and to say that an oval thing appears oval from a certain perspective is not to say that each is the same in appearance.

Why would anyone think that F's use of 'appears' might have a different implication from the one that Austin can sanction? Even mature perceivers do make errors. Suppose, for example, that through inattention to the fact that there is a round coin before her, F looks at it from a twenty-five-degree angle and judges that there is something oval before her.[8] Here the account of how she makes such a mistake is crucial. Ayer, Austin's opponent in this famous debate, would say that it is because she has the same *sensation* (of which more shortly) when she sees the round coin at the angle in question, as the sensation she would have if she were seeing a genuinely oval thing from an angle in which it looks oval, that she mistakenly judges that there is an oval thing before her.[9] Here, when she says she sees something that appears oval, she is allegedly *not* implying that she knows better. Thus the argument of no intrinsic difference gains a foothold.

In response, Austin would claim that this is not the correct description of the case. Rather, it is precisely because of inattention to her surroundings that she makes such a mistaken judgment. To put the point another way, F would never agree, if she knew the context and were asked 'What is the shape that you see?,' that she is seeing an oval shape. For she knows as well as any philosopher that there are no shapes without things that have them, and there is nothing oval in her vicinity.[10] It is not because she sees an oval shape – let alone, something oval – that she makes a mistaken judgment, but because she is mistaken about the entire perceptual situation. To take a similar case: the reason that Descartes mistakenly believes that dreams can sometimes give us experiences exactly like those in waking life is that he begins with the *judgment* one might make in the dream – for example, I see the Pope – and concludes that there must be some sense presentation in the dream that is exactly like the real Pope would present in waking life. But it is the very *nature* of a dream that we can make such judgments from experiences that are not at all exactly similar to waking experiences; that's what a dream *does*. Analogous to the dream context is the waking context in which one is not aware of all the conditions of perception, as is the case with F in the present example.

Let us take one more possible case of error. Suppose that F makes a more insidious error. Believing she is seeing a round coin from a twenty-five-degree angle, F judges that she is seeing something round that looks oval, but in fact she is seeing something oval from the angle at which genuinely oval things appear oval. Is this a case more favourable for Ayer? It certainly seems so, since it seems hard to understand F's mistake unless there is no intrinsic difference between seeing an oval thing from an angle at which it looks oval and seeing a round thing at an angle from which it looks oval. As we understand him, however, Austin would again deny that the situation has been accurately described. A genuinely oval thing looks different from the angle at which F is in fact looking at it (twenty-five degrees to the horizon) than a round coin looks at that angle. If one does make the mistake in question, it is not because there is no intrinsic difference between the two situations, but because F is not paying attention to the situation *as a whole*.

One reason that Ayer, and so many others, have been entranced by the 'no intrinsic difference' argument is that he in fact believes there is another way of describing the perceptual situation besides T's, in so far as T is characterized as knowing the laws of perspective, and so on. T's argument of no intrinsic difference is alleged to show this, as follows: Once one realizes that one is presented with the same perceptual quality on the two different occasions on which one sees the round coin that looks oval and the oval thing that looks oval, one can abstract the seen shapes out of perspectival context. If that is true, if one can consider the shapes as presented independently of their context of presentation, then why can't we abstract the shapes, so to speak, and realize that a person either ignorant of or ignoring perspective and context can do exactly the same thing? That is, why can't one adopt a point of view on perception that *begins*, not with physical objects, but with these shapes, colours, and so on, which the 'no intrinsic difference' argument has shown must exist? This is the first-person, phenomenalistic, perspective. Once we appreciate F's perspective, Ayer thinks, we see that it indeed aids and abets T's argument, because it appears to be *independent* of it. In other words, the allegedly independent phenomenalistic move by F, and the 'no intrinsic difference' argument by T mutually reinforce each other. If one can begin as F now wants to, in speaking of phenomenal shapes, then this reinforces T's contention that there can be situations of no intrinsic difference between diverse presentations. On the other hand, if one begins with T's argument of no intrinsic difference, then one sees that there are phenomenal shapes that can be abstracted from the perceptual context of physical objects and perspective. The common thread is that there exist phenomenal qualities.

If the 'no intrinsic difference' argument works, then, given the reasoning applied above, the first-person point of view seems initially plausible. The 'abstraction' argument indicates that there might be a way of describing perceptual experience unfettered by knowledge of the laws of perspective and using a vocabulary made up solely of predicates of size, shape, colour, and the like.[11] Historically there has been a peculiar symbiotic relationship between F's and T's points of view – surely the phenomenalistic approach by F could not work if the 'no intrinsic difference' argument failed, and conversely. F's point of view almost certainly would never have occurred to anyone without the argument of no intrinsic difference.[12] It is T's argument, surely, that suggests there may be a mode of description in terms of a judgment-free vocabulary. None the less, if the 'no intrinsic difference' argument is successful, F's point of view is logically independent of T's.

To see this more clearly, let us suppose that someone (a follower of Ayer) objects to our characterization of the first-person situation as follows: there is a genuine first-person point of view that does *not*, logically or psychologically, import a 'no intrinsic difference' argument from third-person point of view. Just concentrate on *sensation*: one sees colours, hears sounds, and so on, and this is surely commonsensical and not fraught with any philosophical difficulties. As we have seen, the argument of no intrinsic difference does seem to indicate that this can be done. For if one can genuinely abstract, say, the perception of a shape from the context of the perception, the abstraction would not be possible unless one could experience a shape independently of what else one knows (or fails to know) about the perceptual situation one is in. So, when one is in fact seeing a round coin that looks oval, and perhaps at the same time a really oval object, one simply reports one's *sensations* – which are that one is seeing two instances of oval.

But this distinction between sensation and either perception or perceptual judgment is itself highly suspect, tempting as it is to associate sounds with ears, and colours and shapes with eyes. Indeed, we think it can be plausibly argued that the entire distinction between sensation and perception, far from being commonsensical, is a metaphysical reflection of the desire, which stems from third-person point of view, to account for perceptual variation. After all, one could say, one sees shaped things, not merely shapes, and one hears the sounds of trains, and so on.

To say that one can describe the round coin that looks oval and the really oval thing as having no intrinsic difference in so far as the *experience* of each is concerned is therefore to force artificially a point of view which makes no sense apart from its third-person background. Without an argument of 'no intrinsic difference,' which, as we have seen, rests on the assumption that there are physical objects that appear to us in certain ways, there would be no reason whatever to think that there are independently describable sensations of qualities from the point of view of their epistemological priority. There is, in other words, a dialectical motive behind the argument of no intrinsic difference which equally informs the phenomenalistic starting-point – namely, to account fully for what one is presented with in sense perception with an eye towards justifying knowledge claims. But, as Goodman argues, claims about how our experience really is are highly suspect; the best one can do if one wishes to begin one's discussion of perception with sensible qualities is simply to postulate their existence and see where we get using that postulation; no claim that these qualities are really what we experience need be made. On the other hand, if there were a privileged position, as Austin would argue there is, it is the one taken by everyday common sense. We know the laws of perspective and how *physical objects* appear to us under different conditions; it is our perspective on our own perceptions and, by analogy, the perceptions of others as well.

Beginning a discussion of F's position with sensations is thus fraught with difficulties. Besides, there is a problem in claiming that one is presented with sensible qualities *alone*. Even though Berkeley often speaks this way, he is a rabid anti-Platonist, and in a certain sense a nominalist. Qualities cannot exist alone; they must be qualities *of* something. Berkeley insists that we are aware of blue somethings, of square somethings.

Indeed, proponents of the 'no intrinsic difference' argument given from T's point of view will wonder, given perceptual experiences of the same quality as described above, what it is that is appearing the same way under two sets of conditions, since at most one can be the coin. The answer to this is, usually, a phenomenal entity, a sense datum, in *both* presentations, and not – as one might be tempted to say, given their knowledge of Berkeley – an idea (we shall explain this difference shortly). So, whether one uses first- or third-person point of view, the result is not merely the experience of a quality but a quality *of something*.

The introduction into the debate of the *something* which instantiates the qualities of phenomenal experience adds new ontological significance to the controversy. To F, when *starting* from the first-person point of view, there is alleged to be no intrinsic difference between reality and mere appearance. Seeing something round is as real to her as seeing something oval, having a hallucination of something oval is no different to her from seeing something oval. That is, with respect to immediate content alone, F's *initial* descriptions of what she sees are not (so the argument goes) infected with judgments imported from the third-person point of view. Since there are no judgments, there is allegedly no possibility of error in F's reports, and no discrepancy between appearance and reality. Thus, F will not say 'There is a round coin' when presented with something round, but merely that she sees something round.

But this is not the end of the matter. After all, both F and T claim that there is a *something* that has the property in question, a something round, a something oval. Their report has a structure like that of a judgment. Granted we are not (necessarily) speaking about physical objects; we are speaking of a something that has a property. Doesn't that make the situation *parallel* to that of physical objects, where we have an object that we judge has properties and, in making that judgment, run into problems of perceptual variation? Then, why doesn't the problem of perceptual variation crop up all over again?

To avoid this problem, proponents of sense data insist that the claim expressed by 'this (sense datum) is round' is not a judgment, but merely an expression of the fact that properties cannot exist or appear alone; they must be individuated in some way.[13] The '*this*' *is a mere individuator* and not a subject about which we make judgments. If one were to claim that such an individuator could continue to exist through several perceptions, that might introduce the problem that it could be seen from another perspective, and we would be back in T's soup. Classical phenomenalism is thus seen to be, as Austin suspected, totally motivated by the problems of perceptual variation.

If there is no possibility of error with respect to sense data, then sense data are surely very different from physical objects. The next move is crucial. One could start from T's viewpoint and end a representationalist, with sense data as ideas in the mind representing physical objects, as Russell does in *The Problems of Philosophy*. The move to make sense data mental is quite natural, given that one starts with physical objects, that is, reality, and given that the ontological status of appearances, sense data, is contrasted with that reality.[14] If, on the other hand, one begins from F's first-person perspective, one must now *reconstruct* physical objects from sense data. Among other things, this means that the problem of perceptual variation must now be *reintroduced* and solved at the phenomenal level. We note, however, that, beginning from F's perspective, given the logical independence of F's point of view from T's, there is no implication that sense data are mental or physical entities. Rather, we are in the position of Goodman in *The Structure of Appearance*, neutral phenomenalism, where the mental and the physical are categories constructed from patterns of sense data.[15] Our point is that, logically, F's point of view does not automatically land one in a theory of ideas.

Logically, then, Berkeley could not justifiably introduce sense data as ideas solely from F's point of view. Does he, then, categorize sense data as mental because he believes, as Russell does, that they thereby solve the problem of perceptual variation? The peculiarity of such a move now becomes apparent. A physical sphere will be reconstructed, as Berkeley would have it, as a collection of mind-dependent sense data. But of course he, too, must account for, and then solve, the problem of perceptual variation, just as a neutral phenomenalist must. A round coin must still be able to look oval, and an oval coin must be able to look oval. Each will be a collection of sense data that includes oval individuals. 'Wild data,' for example, from dreams, will be assigned a different kind from the data constituting physical objects.[16] But if all this is so, one wonders, why couldn't one have solved these problems by analysing physical objects this way? If we are going to allow 'appearances' as part of the real coin, we could do that without the move to a strange limbo of sense data as *ideas*. In so far as the problem of perceptual variation goes, starting with sense data classified as ideas is no better than starting with physical objects as collections of momentarily existing entities. *The moral of the tale is that, giving Berkeley the benefit of the doubt, his classification of sensible qualities as ideas does not rest on the argument from perceptual variation.*

The history of philosophy shows that many philosophers who *use* either third- or what they believe to be first-person point of view land in one of the three dilemmas of representationalism, idealism, or scepticism. The reason for italicizing 'use' is that many philosophers begin their epistemological stances by trying to solve an *information* problem: how do we get perceptual information from the external world? Descartes, Locke, and Berkeley wish to solve this problem. Thus, the argument from perceptual *variation* is, very often, part of a larger argument about perceptual *information* in which first or third person, or both, plays a vital role. We wish now to display the connection between the problems of perceptual variation and information.

Philosophers land in sceptical or representational problems by refusing to give up the view that there is an independent world, but switching when convenient to a first-person point of view. The switch is not surprising, considering the temptation to make T one who knows the facts of science, and so on, but also one who knows what is seen from the inside and thus one who can ignore the facts of science. Looked at from F's first-person point of view, the argument goes, one does not describe the situation of looking at the round coin from a particular angle as seeing a coin that appears oval, but rather as seeing something oval. If T takes these reports seriously, and does not translate F's description into appearance talk, then T, empathizing with F, will be tempted to say that, although he knows the coin is round, F is seeing something oval. Neither this something nor its shape, from T's point of view, can be identical with the coin and its shape. The switch, in other words, immediately engenders intermediaries of some sort: third person tells T that F is not seeing the coin as it really is; first person tells T that F is seeing *something*. The inevitable conclusion is that there is something to be seen that stands between F and the coin. This is the view that Russell so perfectly outlines in *The Problems of Philosophy*. Russell's argument, though, at least according to some, echoes Berkeley's in the *Dialogues* and Locke's in the *Essay*.[17] Such an argument seems clearly self-defeating. Russell ends by denying that we have any access to the physical world that is not inferential (at best); yet the argument from perceptual variation, which gets us into that position, clearly depends upon a full-blown third-person point of view. What misleads Russell is the unnoticed switch he makes to first-person point of view; he thus acts as if he has arrived at the sense-data view independently of perceptual variation when, of course, he has not done so at all.

Berkeley greatly facilitates his move to idealism by using a first-person point of view. But as we have seen, he never justifies his claim that we are directly aware of sensations or sensible qualities as opposed to, say, trees and trains. He is thus, in our view, implicitly appealing to the argument from perceptual variation and the claim of 'no intrinsic difference.' Berkeley believes he can begin from a pure first-person point of view and reconstruct the existence of the physical world later.[18] He treats a central claim in the *Dialogues*, that we are directly aware of sensible qualities, as if it is a piece of common sense that needs no argument. Indeed, he uses this assumption to *introduce* the arguments from perceptual variation. Given our arguments above, this represents confusion on Berkeley's part, since 'perceptual variation' arguments are what suggest F's point of view to begin with.[19] Obviously, Berkeley cannot explicitly make the same use of perceptual variation and the switch from third- to first-person as does Russell, since Russell ends by still acknowledging a set of independently existing physical objects. Indeed, as we have argued elsewhere, despite appearances from the *Dialogues*, Berkeley uses the supposition that there is an independently existing physical world to force a *reductio* via the argument against representationalism. If there is an independently existing physical world, then the argument against representationalism shows we can never know it. Since we do know much about ordinary objects, there cannot be such an independently existing physical world. So the third-person point of view, with its attendant premise of a physical world whose ontological status differs from that of sensible qualities, is purged by the argument against representationalism.

Once the *reductio* is given, why still hold that we are directly aware of sensible qualities, the very entities seemingly posited by his enemies? As we suggested earlier, Berkeley does not see that his extensive use of 'perceptual variation' arguments in the *Dialogues* is the real reason behind his identification of the directly perceived as sensible qualities because he believes he is using the arguments against the primary–secondary quality distinction. Explicitly, that is what he is doing. Implicitly, he is using perceptual variation – with its third-person assumptions – to identify the directly perceived with what we have argued is an artificially constructed category of sensation. In other words, given Berkeley's extensive use of perceptual variation arguments in the *Dialogues*, we believe he has the motivation for positing a category of sensations of sensible qualities; he has a motivation for saying we hear a sound rather than saying we hear the sound *of a train*.

Notice what Berkeley has shown here, assuming that the argument against representationalism works, and even that we are directly aware of sensible qualities. He has shown that sensible qualities cannot be intermediaries between a perceiver and a physical world, which intermediaries must themselves be grasped by another act of awareness, for that would lead to regress. He has not shown, however, that sensible qualities are mind-dependent. The argument against representationalism is perfectly compatible with the following *scenario*: sensible qualities are mind-independent 'parts' of physical objects and, as such, they cause, via the normal causal chain, a *perception* of *them*. Thus, in order to accommodate the obvious necessity for some causal connection between a perceiver and the perceived, but to cut off the problems engendered by intermediaries, the effect of the causal chain must be an act of awareness and not the existence of some datum, for example, a sense datum or other entity that must be grasped for information. Such a position would almost certainly invoke some sort of *intentionalist* stance.

Berkeley believes, as many do, that in order to have information about objects, there must be something that carries that information. But if what the information is about is external to and independent of the mind, there must be *intermediaries* which carry information – and there cannot be intermediaries without scepticism. Berkeley does not recognize a Cartesian way out as a possibility because intentional entities – which we have argued earlier are Descartes's crucial innovation in philosophy of mind – do not have the requisite features to represent anything, since they are not like what they represent. Yet if they are like what they represent, there is trouble anyway. That is the *reductio* that Berkeley presents as the argument against representationalism. So the solution is not to bring information about the object into the mind, but to bring the object itself into the mind. Berkeley sees no alternative to idealism, in great part because he buys the argument of his opponents that independently existing entities, that is, entities existing independently of perception, cannot be known without intermediaries.

Descartes, by invoking intentional mental representations, believes he escapes Berkeley-like criticism (Locke, however, appears to be trapped in Berkeley's dilemma). Furthermore, despite his use of the 'dream' problem, Descartes himself is never in the grip of the 'perceptual variation' argument. His concern is a much deeper one, with the truth conditions for ideas. It is not that perceptual variation could not lead one to intentional entities; the switch from third- to first-person facilitated by the 'no intrinsic difference' argument does not *inevitably* lead to sense data. But Descartes's approach begins and remains strictly in line with pure third-person: the facts and laws of nature. If we may put it some-what fancifully, we see Descartes as implicitly arguing that, even if we always saw the world as it is – that is, round coins appeared round from any point of view, and so on – there would still be an information prob-lem that needs solution. There is a physical object as described by Gali-leo. The physical object, together with the conditions of perception, the sense organs, the brain, and the like, produces a causal process ending in a change in the perceiver, an awareness of something. Even if we assume that we always see things as they are, *how* this works, how cor-rect information is carried and processed, still needs to be addressed. Now the logic of the argument against representationalism looms, and Descartes, we believe, anticipates it, and makes mental representations intrinsically representational, that is, representational by their vary nature. These entities are what Descartes calls 'ideas.' We thus have a radically new sort of entity that calls for a radically new sort of home, mental substance. Note, however, that the move to ideas is the final step in the argument, not the first: first-person experience is explained, not invoked. Berkeley begins with first-person; he starts with sensible quali-ties. Once he brings the likeness and unlikeness arguments to bear against the assumptions of representationalism, idealism is but a step away.

In summary: the argument from perceptual variation alone cannot lead to idealism in a logical sense, nor does Berkeley think that it can. Rather, his arguments rest on the assumption of sensible qualities as the beginning point for solving the problem of information. This assump-tion does indeed depend on perceptual variation, but idealism depends upon a misguided attempt to show that perceptual information can be provided only by the very entities the information is alleged to be about. It should be obvious that if one has to bring chairs into the mind to get information about them, something is radically wrong. We have, in this chapter, tried to show that the 'perceptual variation' argument, while closely tied to idealism, not only does not establish it, but has alternative interpretations that will not even allow Berkeley to establish with cer-tainty the existence of sensible qualities. Without them, idealism is much more than a step away.

Epilogue

Descartes has often been classified as an indirect realist. Aquinas, it is sometimes said, is a direct realist. But, as every philosopher knows, giving exact meanings to the notions of direct and indirect realism is problematic. We hope to provide meanings for these terms that will reveal crucial differences between Descartes, on the one hand, and Hume and Berkeley, on the other. But whether one has a Cartesian or a Berkeleyan sense of direct realism, the purpose of trying to be one is the same: to solve the information problem, and thereby to avoid scepticism. The key to our explication is the idea of the intentional entity that we introduced in our discussion of Cartesian semantics.

Russell is an excellent candidate for one well-known explication of 'indirect realist.' Given the causal process that occurs between physical object and brain state, and because of an argument based on perceptual variation, Russell believes that what is produced by the brain state is a propertied entity, a sense datum which one directly perceives.[1] On the basis of this datum, one makes a judgment about what exists in the physical world. But Russell candidly admits that, given the nature of sense data, the existence of the physical world is, at best, only inductively probable or, as he sometimes puts it, the best hypothesis as to why we have sense data at all, let alone the particular ones that we do have. Given the structure of Russell's view, knowledge of the physical world is indirect in the sense that it is inferential.

Obviously, Russell is a candidate for Berkeley's 'likeness' argument: if sense data are like physical objects, then either (a) they too need intermediaries and so are not directly perceived or (b) physical objects do not need intermediaries and there is no need for sense data. Consider (a). As we have read the problem, the sense datum must be assigned a semantic function. To do this, one must grasp the properties of the sense datum as a representative which is like what it represents, and assign those properties of the representation a semantics: this property of the representation stands for this property of the thing, and so on. Now, it may seem mysterious as to how this problem arises here – after all, there cannot be a physical process of 'seeing' the sense datum in the same way as there was a seeing of something which produced the sense datum in the first place. But we believe this is in essence the whole Fodor–Dennett point. If one did have to grasp the properties of the sense datum in order to first assign it a semantics, there would have to be a new causal process culminating in the production of an information-carrying intermediary and an interpretation of *it* by a homunculus. This is just where the repeat of the original problem, of how we get information about an object in the environment, becomes manifest. So, in the Fodor–Dennett view, there just cannot be such a homunculus with the self-same abilities as the perceiver. Here, we have argued, Descartes makes his semantic innovation.

Whether sense data are like little two-dimensional versions of three-dimensional objects, or whether they have properties that three-dimensional objects could not have (e.g., colours), they are ontologically too similar to serve as intrinsic semantic vehicles. As we have argued, the whole point of postulating the existence of intentional entities is to avoid the problems engendered by a sense-data view.[2] If no semantics need be assigned, then we do not get a homunculus problem. Of course, one does have to grasp the properties of the *intentional* entity that Descartes believes serves the function of a semantic object. But because being aware of the intentional entity is the same as knowing what it is about, nothing has to be *done* with that entity to *produce* understanding; a direct awareness that is like a 'searchlight' will do.[3] This, then, is a sense of 'direct realism'; Descartes does not have intermediary problems like Russell. Knowledge of entities outside our minds is direct, in the sense that the semantics for intentional entities guarantees the existence of the extramental things of which we are aware by means of them.

The searchlight metaphor can help us understand how Descartes's view contrasts with that of Berkeley and Hume. Berkeley and Hume are sometimes called direct realists; indeed, this is how Berkeley describes himself when he claims he is saving common sense from the scepticism of Descartes and Locke. What does direct realism amount to here? In chapter 7 we argued that, because of his worry about intermediaries and his failure to recognize intentional entities as legitimate, Berkeley brings into the mind not representatives of objects, but the objects themselves. This, he feels, is the only way to secure knowledge of the physical world, to solve the information problem. But there is no obvious search-light that illuminates these objects; rather, as we have seen – and discuss again below – objects illumine themselves. They are at once searchlights and what the lights are upon. Berkeley pays a high price for this version of direct realism.

The cost can be measured as follows: Berkeley and Hume believe we are directly aware of sensible qualities. Thus, one must be directly aware of trees and chairs and tables, in the sense that, at a given moment, one is directly aware of properties which are part of the much larger bundle that constitutes physical objects. How Berkeley and Hume secure this larger bundle need not concern us here. The point is that their problems in reconstruction are now the same as those of any twentieth-century phenomenalist in so far as they are forced to reconstruct the entire phys-ical world from the immediate objects of sense. This means, for example, that the facts of perceptual variation and the causal theory of perception must somehow be reintroduced and solved within the context of their version of direct realism without also reintroducing the problems which drove the world 'inside' in the first place.

How such a feat is to be accomplished is far from obvious. Berkeley, for example, already has a category of the mental with his invocation of mental substances. We have seen that sensible qualities are alleged to be mental in a sense derived from the category of mental substance, since as *ideas* they inhere in such substances. But these very same entities, sen-sible qualities, must also constitute the category of the physical. Of course, commonsensically, Berkeley knows that ordinary objects are not always as they appear. How will he give credence to that fact? Good-man, for example, might do this by distinguishing, as we have claimed earlier, between sensible qualities that are mere parts of a bundle and sensible qualities that are qualities of the bundle. A part may exist only at a moment; a genuine quality shows a pattern over many moments. Given *his* direct realism, Berkeley can solve perceptual variation without invoking any of the arguments that lead fatally to sense data of the Rus-sell kind. So far, perhaps, so good.

But there is a more difficult problem to solve before their version of direct realism is viable, and this problem exposes a fatal flaw. Common-sensically, an ordinary object interacts with our sense organs to produce an awareness of it in a perceiver. No adequate theory of perception can escape this fact: this is in effect the information problem. As we have seen, trying to deal with it from third-person point of view also leads, in Berkeley's eyes, to fatal consequences. The 'likeness' argument destroys any view of mental representation which makes those representations like what they are about, and Berkeley simply does not recognize semantic objects in the Cartesian sense. Sensible qualities need no intermediaries to be grasped. Let us try once more to explain how Berkeley tries to maintain this.

Putting the point suggestively, we hope (if not totally accurately), if sensible qualities are in the mind, why would one need intermediaries to grasp them? There they are, ready to be grasped. Yet, if they do not need intermediaries, and if there is correspondingly no causal connection between sensible qualities and the mind that grasps them, then a cardinal principle of common sense has been violated. Here, as we have argued above, Berkeley does a sleight of hand by means of which he doubly fools himself. If we are dealing genuinely with sensible qualities, if we are to construct physical objects from them, and if these qualities are, given certain patterns of them, to qualify physical objects, these qualities cannot be qualities of the mind. As we know quite well from section 49 of the *Principles*, Berkeley claims the mind is not square when one sees a square thing. But then in what sense are such sensible qualities mental, capable of being in the mind as ideas, or in any way qualifying mental substance? Indeed, given sensible qualities as constituents of physical objects, one certainly wonders why the information problem does not start all over again.

As we have argued, Berkeley could solve the problem if he had acts with intrinsically intentional properties, but he believes – mistakenly we think – that acts would engender the Fodor–Dennett problems.[4] What he does not see is that without them, he has a different version of those problems – he indeed violates the cardinal principle that any theory of perception must follow: there must be an awareness in the perceiver of the object of perception, and this awareness must in some way be a carrier of usable information.[5]

What to do? Berkeley takes the heroic (or foolhardy) step of bringing the object itself into the mind. But now, given that sensible qualities are mental, depropertied as it were, they cannot be constituents of physical objects. That is, given section 49, if sensible qualities are mental, they can no longer be qualities of physical objects. Thus, he can no longer reconstruct physical objects from these mental entities. Indeed, to maintain, as he does in section 49, that sensible qualities are in the mind by way of idea is truly an attempt to have it both ways – as if a sensible quality is encapsulated in something, which 'thing' is a property of the mind, even if its 'content' is not. Berkeley begins to sound like Descartes, except that Descartes knows – as we have argued – that such encapsulated entities are not properties of anything; that is, one cannot use such content to reconstruct physical objects, but merely to 'refer' to them. If we now think commonsensically of the fact that a physical object causes an awareness in us of it, it is hard to see how Berkeley will escape the absurdity that ordinary objects literally cause themselves as ideas of themselves.

In Hume this absurdity is further hidden by the fact that strings of sensible qualities make up physical objects, and that the members of these strings occur in different relations to other items, for example, ideas of sensation, impressions of reflection, to make up the mind. The absurdity is that a sensible quality as member of a physical bundle is also a member of a mental one; that is, the quality must cause in the mind an impression of it, but that impression *is* it, in different relations to other entities.

Our account of Berkeley here stands in sharp contrast to the Inherence Account which we both once embraced.[6] The problem with this account is that it totally ignores the information problem. Arguing that Berkeley's first step towards idealism is the argument against the existence of matter, it sees sensible qualities as dangling in midair, in need of an ontological home. The question is, why not give them a home in physical objects? The Inherence Account simply claims that Berkeley gets confused here because he thinks that sensible qualities, being qualities, must be qualities of something and, with an unsure grasp on the notion of predication owing to the persistence of the substance tradition, he predicates them to the only substance left to him – namely, the mind. But we believe his confusion is deeper. The move to the mind is not because he has an unsure grasp on the category of quality, but because he has an unsure grasp on the concept of grasping, that is, on the information problem, how information is grasped. Once one sees that clearly, the collapse of the act–object distinction, that collapse which so inspired Moore, can be seen in its true light.[7]

Notes

Introduction

1 René Descartes, *The Philosophical Writings of Descartes*, 2 vols. Trans. John Cottingham, Robert Stoothoff, and Dugald Murdoch, vol. 1, 303–4: hereinafter cited as CSM1 and CSM2. Since CSM cross-references Charles Adams and Paul Tannery, eds., *Oeuvres de Descartes* (Paris: J. Vrin 1964–76), we do not include references to it.

2 Somewhat surprisingly, the richer view of content is also in 'Comments on a Certain Broadsheet,' at CSM1, 304. For a discussion of the range of the notion of innateness see Robert Merrihew Adams, 'Where Do Our Ideas Come From – Descartes vs. Locke, 77–8.

3 We hope to sound the rest of them in later work.

4 A symptom of this failure is the contemporary eschewing of the terminology of idealism and – in its classical sense – realism.

5 CSM1, 152ff.

1: Machines, Meaning, and the Theory of Ideas

1 George S. Boolos and Richard C. Jeffrey, *Computability and Logic*, 2d ed., 21.

2 See Alan Hausman, 'Review of Watson's *The Breakdown of Cartesian Metaphysics*.'

3 Early functionalists claimed that functionalism is neutral between traditional materialism and dualism, so that the functions that constitute the mental could be performed by spiritualistic stuff. But this just shows that functionalists are unclear about the traditional view. We shall argue that the hallmark of mind for Descartes was the intentionality of thought, and that intentionality is irreducible. This intentionality is also the hallmark of the homunculus

theory that functionalism eschews. So, in arguing against the homunculus, functionalists eliminate what we believe to be any plausible concept of the non-physical mind. In other words, to allow mental functions to be instantiated in non-physical stuff is to allow homunculi back into one's philosophy of mind, which, we assume, the early functionalists don't really want to do. See John Searle's *The Rediscovery of the Mind*. We are certainly in close agreement with Searle's critiques of current philosophy of mind, but Searle would not think that Descartes needs a non-physical mind to do justice to intentionality.

4 See Daniel C. Dennett, *Brainstorms*, ch. 7, especially 119ff., and Jerry A. Fodor, 'The Mind–Body Problem.' Functionalism has come a long way since Fodor and Dennett wrote the passages that we consider here. But their more recent work is not our concern; we are interested only in the initial contrasts they draw between their own positions and how they see the tradition before them. Similar comments can be made about current work in support of materialism and its attempts to refute traditional theories of mind. That is not to say, however, that these early positions are not in some sense basic, so that bringing to light alternative theories from the seventeeth century, as we shall, might prove useful even to recent work in the philosophy of mind.

5 See Searle, *The Rediscovery of the Mind*.

6 There is by now a vast literature on folk psychology and its virtues and vices. For a particularly interesting set of discussions see William G. Lycan, ed., *Mind and Cognition: A Reader*, sec 6.

7 Descartes and other idea theorists would not use these terms. They would talk instead of ideas, awareness, and so on. We will speak a good deal more of this in later chapters.

8 Bertrand Russell, *Introduction to Mathematical Philosophy*, 181ff.

9 Nelson Goodman, *Languages of Art*, xiii. Goodman makes clear throughout the book that, although he uses class talk for convenience, he could translate into nominalistic discourse if necessary. The implication is that class talk is not only simpler but also intelligible in its own right.

10 Fodor, 'The Mind–Body Problem,' 119.

11 For our purposes, we think it useful to make a distinction between common-sense folk psychology and its extension into a psychological theory, for example, Freud's, much like G.E. Moore distinguishes between common-sense beliefs about trees and scientific extensions of such beliefs by biologists, and ultimately physicists. Biology and physics may correct some of our ordinary beliefs, but a core must remain or there is nothing for biology to do; the same goes for everyday folk psychology and its extensions into (allegedly) scientific theories. This is one major bone of contention between the

Churchlands and functionalist proponents of folk psychology. See Paul M. Churchland, *Matter and Consciousness*, 26ff. and 43ff.

12 In his *Scientific American* essay ('The Mind–Body Problem'), Fodor tries to illustrate the difference between functionalism and behaviourism by analogy to two Coke machines. Both dispense a Coke for ten cents. The mentalistic machine has interdefined states S1 and S2. S1 is the state the machine is in if, given a nickel, it dispenses nothing but proceeds to S2, or, given a dime, it dispenses a Coke and stays in S1. S2 is the state the machine is in if, given a nickel, it dispenses a Coke and returns to S1, and, given a dime, it dispenses a Coke and a nickel and goes back to S1. But, says Fodor, only a machine that dispenses a Coke for a dime would satisfy a behaviourist, presumably because the more complex machine has interdefined inner states, which at least a Skinnerian would abjure. But this example fails. Fodor himself admits that what the mentalistic machine's program comes to is dispensing a Coke for a dime or dispensing a Coke and a nickel for a nickel and a dime or, upon being given a nickel only, doing nothing. Surely a behaviourist can easily observe this behaviour and read off the corresponding functions without any pejorative reference to inner states. Indeed, given the telling 'inverted spectrum' case (of which we make much in later chapters), mental content seems to be a function of input and output relations: since a person who is exposed to red light waves and experiences a green *quale* may behave just as someone exposed to the same light waves and who experiences a red *quale*, many functionalists would claim that there is no difference in mental states, but merely in the mode of representation. Given such problems, early functionalism sees much closer to behaviourism than its proponents care to admit.

2: Descartes's Semantic Intentions

1 CSM1, 304.

2 See Richard A. Watson, *The Breakdown of Cartesian Metaphysics*. The failure of Cartesian semantics, given Descartes's distinction between mind and body, is the central theme of Watson's book.

3 Arthur Danto, 'The Representational Character of Ideas and the Problem of the External World': hereinafter cited as RCI.

4 We ignore for now the fact that, in the *Meditations*, Descartes clearly indicates that judgments, not ideas, are the vehicles of truth and falsity. See Third Meditation, CSM2, 26. See also Margaret Wilson's discussion in *Descartes*, especially 109ff. We shall, however, return to this point later; also see note 10, below.

5 RCI, 288.

6 Ibid., 292.

7 Richmond H. Thomason, *Symbolic Logic*, 241ff. We are not maintaining that this semantical picture is neatly drawn anywhere in Descartes's work. Our interpretation is an *idealization* which we feel fits many important texts and makes sense of many others. Nor are we claiming that an assignment of values for the simples is made by the perceiver, as we discuss later in this chapter. Our point is that, however a representation obtains its semantics, the semantics of the complexes are a function of the semantics of its simples.

8 First Meditation, CSM2, 13–14.

9 This distinction is made quite clearly in Descartes's early work, as well as in the *Meditations*. For our purposes, whether Descartes changes his mind about which entities are simple is not important. What is important is that some entities are taken as simple and others as complexes whose constituents are simples. See *Rules for the Direction of the Mind*, CSM1, Rule XII, especially 43ff.

10 We do not say that each simple idea is *about* such an entity beyond one's own ideas, since we will soon distinguish between the meaning of an idea and what it is about. We are, for now, ignoring the difference between describing an idea by a predicate term and by a sentence, and the difference between sense ideas and the ideas reflecting the judgments we make on the basis of these sense ideas. We fill in these gaps in chapter 4.

11 We will not argue here that Aquinas's theory is not an intentional one (see our discussion in chapter 6, however); we merely point out that, in Aquinas's view, the object perceived shares something with the perception of it – namely, a form, the so-called sensible species. But in Descartes's view, the idea with objective reality does not share something with that of which it is an idea. See *Optics*, CSM1, 153, 154, 164ff. For a characterization of Aquinas, see Anthony Lisska, 'Axioms of Intentionality in Aquinas' Theory of Knowledge.'

12 *Optics*, CSM1, 165. The entire passage, of which this quotation is a small part, is of crucial importance to our argument.

13 Besides marking adjectival uses of technical terms, we often use quotation marks throughout the book as red flags: the use of the quoted word needs explication. We try to provide these when it is possible but, as every philosopher knows, such explications are, unfortunately, not always possible.

14 There is a continuing controversy over whether Descartes embraced a transference model even in case of body–body causation. See Thomas A. Lennon's 'Philosophical Commentary,' 810ff., and Louis E. Loeb, *From Descartes to Hume*, 126ff. and 210ff.

15 See Sixth Meditation, CSM2, 56–7.

16 In our discussion of intentionality in this book, we are deeply indebted to Gustav Bergmann's work on the subject. See especially his 'Intentionality' and 'Acts.'

17 This identification is admittedly controversial, given what Descartes says in the Third Meditation about secondary qualities. We discuss this point in detail in chapter 3.

18 CSM2, 29.

19 CSM1, 198.

20 CSM2, 28.

21 It is not open to Descartes to claim that, even if ordinary physical objects do not casually transfer some likeness to ideas, God could, at a given moment, produce in us an idea which, as it were, means the tree – a kind of occasionalism. As we argue below, if God invests the idea with intrinsic meaning, he must use exemplars to do this; if he does not so invest the idea, we still need a semantics for it. This does not show, of course, that occasionalism cannot be correct, even under Cartesian principles. We will not, however, take up the subject of why Descartes believes that occasionalism will not work; it is clear that he thinks it won't or innate ideas would not be necessary.

22 Locke is here an interesting case. Are his ideas intentional? If he has intentional ideas, he has no natured mental substance to which to hook them. If he holds a genuine likeness relation between ideas and physical objects, then his ideas cannot be intentional. Stillingfleet's wondering why, in Locke's view, bodies could not think, and Locke's answer that it was possible, can now be seen in a somewhat different light. We can sympathize with Stillingfleet's puzzlement: for in the view that ideas are intentional, and given the substance tradition, Locke is seemingly committed to natured mental entities; in the view that ideas are like physical objects, he is not. Had Locke been able to make good on a notion of the intentionality of ideas, ideas as intrinsically mental, he might also have held that minds are not substances, but collections of such ideas, thereby securing the intrinsically mental without mental substance.

23 Daniel C. Dennett, *Brainstorms*, 119ff.

24 The terminology of syntactic and semantic is ours, not Dennett's.

25 Watson, in *The Breakdown of Cartesian Metaphysics*, suggests that some of Foucher's arguments against Descartes's theory of ideas involve the possibility of an infinite regress of representations. See especially 73ff.

26 *Optics*, CSM1, 167.

27 As we use 'intentional,' a thought is intentional in that it is, by its very nature, *about* something other than itself. Its aboutness is not derived, in

other words, from the *assignment* of an interpretation to it, as one does with a language. Our view of intentionality thus derives from the Meinongian tradition. See Bergmann, 'Intentionality.'

28 The possibility, exploited by some today, of intentional properties that are in some sense physical would not have occurred to philosophers of the seventeenth or early eighteenth centuries, who take the qualities of bodies to be mathematizable. Intentional properties would clearly not fit this mould.

29 Aristotle and Descartes share the view that F is a property of *a* if and only if F inheres in *a*.

30 As we have argued above, such a view would also seem to return us to that of the sensible species, since at least the same kind of property that characterizes objects would now characterize ideas in minds.

31 Third Meditation, CSM2, 28.

32 Ibid., 28–9. See also Replies to the Second Set of Objections, CSM2, 97.

3: The Secularity of the *Meditations*

1 This is the import of our discussion of valuation semantics for ideas, tied to our discussion of intrinsic intentionality. We develop this theme much more in this chapter.

2 Third Meditation, CSM2, 28–9.

3 CSM2, 31. Descartes introduces the notion of eminent containment at CSM2, 28 (see our quotation and discussion in chapter 2).

4 Margaret Wilson, *Descartes*, 107–8. The quote from Descartes comes from CSM2, 31.

5 Third Meditation, CSM2, 28–9.

6 Wilson, *Descartes*, 102. Wilson claims that Descartes seems to mean more than that ideas are of something, 'though it might not be easy to determine exactly how *much* more.'

7 Wilson cites CSM2, 163ff., on 109.

8 Ibid., 110.

9 Indeed, Descartes does seem to maintain in the Third Meditation that he could be the cause of his ideas of both primary and secondary qualities. As we shall show, this is a bogus possibility.

10 If one thinks that Descartes does not put much store in claims about no intrinsic difference between sense presentations, then one cannot explain the 'dream' argument and its sceptical implications.

11 In the case of both the true and the materially false, we are seemingly presented with the instantiation of a property. It is precisely because we seem to

be unable to distinguish the two cases of true and false sense presentations that the notion of the sense datum was invented.

12 See the long quotation which begins chapter 2.

13 See Wilson, *Descartes*, 111–12. Descartes claims that even clear and distinct ideas could be caused by the self. This does not show that no ideas present us with possibilities (Wilson argues, 108, that clear and distinct ideas do present us with genuine possibilities), but rather that we cannot be sure where these possibilities reside. She does not refer to the 'eminent containment' doctrine here, but, as we shall argue, what Wilson is raising is the possibility that they could be eminently contained in us.

14 We shall argue that Descartes's claim that all ideas could be eminently contained by the self is in fact disingenuous. Not only does he show that the idea of God could not be so contained, but the same reasons that the idea of God gets us beyond the circle of ideas hold for at least ideas of primary qualities.

15 The motivation for the primary–secondary quality distinction has long perplexed even Descartes's most sympathetic readers. In our view, a version of that perplexity arises as follows: Once Descartes has recognized the need for innate ideas of colour, which he does in the quotation that begins chapter 2, above, why does he stop from claiming that they are exemplified in the physical world? Perhaps in the *Meditations* he saw that granting them status as innate ideas would lead to just such a question, and he could not bring himself to believe that simple ideas that have a semantics of exemplars could fail to be exemplified. Certainly, as John Cottingham pointed out in a recent paper ('Descartes on Colour'), he can make good on what we believe is a compelling reason for wanting to withhold colours from the material world: how they are caused by brain states whose characteristics are all a function of matter in motion seems inexplicable. Even if one claims that causation of ideas of primary qualities by such brain states is equally inexplicable, Cottingham reasons, correctly we think, that the content of ideas of primaries presents the same sort of qualities as those had by brain states, whereas this is not true of colour sensations. Whatever Descartes's reasons for partially reversing himself in 'Comments on a Certain Broadsheet,' the reversal is at least consistent with other of his claims about ideas: we have many mathematical ideas which may not be instantiated in the physical world. In our view, Descartes's final position on colours need not worry him. There can be non-exemplified exemplars about which we have ideas. In some possible worlds, there would be colours.

16 We are not claiming that the functionalist and sense-data views have the same sort of semantics, at least not in this sense: a sense-data view, like Russell's,

attempts to preserve a hook-up between ideas and things; the hook-up will have the same resultant as Descartes's. There is, as it were, a string that we fix between the thing and its idea. This view obviously runs afoul of the Fodor–Dennett semantic problem. But functionalism also has an extrinsic view of meaning – here, meaning is a function of the relationships between ideas and other ideas, and the functions that manipulate them. The notion of a truth condition is wholly different from that proposed by either Descartes or sense-data theorists. What links the sense-data theorist to the functionalist is that neither can forge a guarantee that there is anything beyond ideas.

17 Functionalists escape their own semantic problem by simply assuming there is such a world. Our ideas are meaningful when we behave in such a way that we do not bump against that world. As we have mentioned previously, this certainly appears to be behaviouristic.

18 Descartes never directly explains why it is that all of us in ordinary life believe that we are directly aware, not of our own ideas, but of the physical world itself. One can see the doctrine of the intentionality of ideas as an attempt at such an explanation: we are, whether we know it or not, presented with ideas; the contents of what are in fact ideas present themselves as the qualities of existing things. That reasoning is the basis of the second sense, (2), of 'as if of things.'

19 As mentioned previously, we must still show how the details of Descartes's semantic scheme works, in terms of how perceptual ideas form the basis of judgments, and how perceptual ideas and judgments derive their meanings from innate ideas.

20 Perhaps one can envision the demon with individuated acts of will, each one correlated to the production of a specific innate idea, but this pattern is not obviously lawful. For lawfulness, the act must be repeatable, which an individual act is not.

21 God's power, or lack of it, over eternal truths has been the subject of much controversy. Harry Frankfurt, in 'Descartes on the Creation of Eternal Truths,' claims that Descartes believes that truths that humans find necessary may not be from God's point of view, but that the goal of the *Meditations* is only to find what it would be rational for us to believe, not what might be 'absolutely' true. This stand has the peculiar result (among many) of rendering the *Meditations* circular from God's point of view, but not ours. See also E.M. Curley's fine discussion of Harry Frankfurt's ('Descartes on the Creation of Eternal Truths') and his own views in 'Descartes on the Creation of the Eternal Truths,' and Richard Kennington's 'The Finitude of Descartes's Evil Genius.' Recently, Jonathan Bennett ('Descartes's Theory of Modality') has argued that the notion of necessary truth in Descartes can best be expli-

cated subjectively: a necessary truth is one whose negation is inconceivable by us. Bennett's entire project is an attempt to preserve Descartes from the charge that, in his view, nothing is absolutely necessary or impossible for God. The result would be disaster for everything else that Descartes holds near and dear. Thus, at least in spirit, Bennett's view is the same as ours, since our argument too is that Descartes's use of the *ex nihilo* principle saves him from the irrational world of the second and third demons.

22 CSM2, 291. For other relevant Cartesian passages see Frankfurt, 'Descartes on the Creation of Eternal Truth,' and Curley, 'Descartes on the Creation of the Eternal Truths.'

23 For corroboration of our point see Calvin Normore, 'Meaning and Objective Being: Descartes and His Sources,' especially 236ff. For discussion of the importance of exemplars (Frankfurt calls them essences) see Frankfurt, 'Descartes on the Creation of Eternal Truths.'

24 For the relevant passages, see the quotes in the first part of this chapter and the latter part of chapter 2.

25 We do not mean, by using the example of the woman and the building, to claim that Descartes unequivocally invokes the *ex nihilo* principle in cases of, say, body–body causation, let alone body–mind interaction. Indeed, whether or not he does use the principle here is very controversial. However, given Descartes's reliance on the logical structure of the Aristotelian substance position, one can envision how, for example, the acorn contains the oak tree 'eminently' – though, of course, Descartes would have to rewrite this story in terms of primary qualities. Or, to turn to Leibniz, he gives a model of how a monad contains all the changes it will manifest 'eminently.'

26 We say 'may not' because, as we shall see in a moment, Descartes does not hold a clear view with respect to the issue of whether exemplars actually exemplify the properties for which they are the model. This is not surprising, given the long history of such problems about exemplars. But whichever way one goes on this, our point is that some version of exemplars is necessary to extend the *ex nihilo* principle to the causation of our ideas.

27 Third Meditation, CSM2, 29.

28 The problem is not necessarily that an archetype that is extended and in the mind of God renders God's mind extended; rather an extended thing is a physical object, and God's mind cannot have such objects as properties.

29 In their discussion of necessary truths and the corresponding essences involved in them, neither Curley nor Frankfurt seems to us to be clear about the issue of the ontological status of essences: as ideas in God's mind or exemplars outside. It is no accident that, after Descartes, Malebranche and Leibniz become enamoured with the idea of possible worlds. As we see it,

Cartesian semantics strongly suggests this notion. If our explication of eminent containment is correct, X eminently contains Y if it has the power to produce Y. Possible worlds are thus the possibilities within the exemplars and their combinations.

30 *Optics*, CSM1, 153.
31 We explain the relation between innate ideas and ideas of sense in chapter 4.

4: Is Hume the Cartesian Evil Demon?

1 *Optics*, CSM1, 165ff.
2 See *Treatise on Man*, CSM1, 106.
3 *Optics*, CSM1, 167. This law will be of some importance in our later discussion of the first evil demon and the possibility this demon raises of systematic deception with respect to the content of our judgments of sense.
4 Nancy Maull's essay 'Cartesian Objects and the Geometrization of Nature' provides a rich set of corroborative detail for our arguments concerning the construction of the sense field.
5 *Optics*, CSM1, 167ff. Obviously there has to be a considerable amount of rather complex 'hardwiring' here, as well as complex connections between brain states and innate ideas, if all these connections are to work as they must. The sphere on the cube must trigger, via its connected brain state, the right innate idea, which in turn produces the correct visual field, which gives rise to the right sort of judgment. The innate geometry which allows us to judge, say, distance from sensations is only one part of this process. Perhaps it is this complexity which, at least in part, fuels Malebranche's rejection of Cartesian innate ideas. See Nicolas Malebranche, *The Search after Truth*, 226–7, and Nicholas Jolley, 'Leibniz and Malebranche on Innate Ideas,' 78ff.

   We speak throughout our discussion here as if the external world consists of macro objects, that is, if Mary's judgment is true, then there is a cube and a sphere. We have mentioned in chapter 2 that Descartes takes the external world to consist of micro objects. For our purposes, the difference does not matter, since what we are trying to develop is a semantics for primary qualities, and primary qualities characterize both macro and micro objects.
6 Maull, 'Cartesian Objects and the Geometrization of Nature,' 23.
7 Ibid., 36.
8 Robert Merrihew Adams, 'Where Do Our Ideas Come From – Descartes *vs.* Locke,' 77.
9 See Alan Hausman, 'Innate Ideas,' and W.T. Stace, *A Critical History of Greek Philosophy*, 279ff.
10 See note 29, chapter 3, above.

11 The problem of individuation has an interesting twentieth-century history, beginning with Russell. A comprehensive set of readings on the subject is provided by Michael Loux in *Universals and Particulars: Readings in Ontology*. That one can provide a semantics for the logical transcriptions of ordinary-language statements without ontological commitment as to what an individual is, is clear from any logic textbook using the techniques of natural deduction. See, for example, Richmond H. Thomason's semantics in *Symbolic Logic*.

12 Malebranche's views are an interesting contrast here. He has a very difficult time distinguishing infinite intelligible extension from physical stuff, the actual world from the possible worlds which he so clearly discusses. Indeed, in Malebranche's view, the only reason we have for believing that there is a physical world is that it says so in Genesis. In our view, this amounts to the claim that we may not need an actual physical world to account fully for the semantics of individual judgments about the physical world. See Nicolas Malebranche, *Dialogues on Metaphysics*, Dialogue VI, and especially 133 and 135.

13 The content of the thought, contrary to Hintikka's interpretation, is thus irrelevant (Jaako Hintikka, '*Cogito Ergo Sum:* Inference or Performance?') But we do not see the *cogito* as an inference, either; at least, it is not an inference from 'there is thinking' to 'there is a thinker,' based on some principle that there cannot be a mode without a substance. Rather, it is because the thinking presents itself as particularized – it is, after all, a particular thought at a particular time – that we know there is a thinker, because the particularity is *presented*. This thinking is a particular thinking because it is the thinking of a particular thinker; the first use of 'particular' ontologically reflects the second. To put the point another way, to say, as Descartes does, that he is aware that he is thinking is to make that thinking – whatever it may be a thinking about – into the content of a second awareness. The content of that second awareness is the particularized thinking about something or other. For a somewhat parallel discussion see Julius R. Weinberg, '*Cogito, Ergo, Sum:* Some Reflections on Mr. Hintikka's Article.'

14 See especially Meditation Six, CSM2, 54, and footnote 2 on that page.

15 Nelson Goodman, *The Structure of Appearance*, 145ff.

16 CSM2, 20.

17 Ibid., 21.

18 One might plausibly argue that the view of a natured – in this case the nature is to be extended – substratum is not the one Locke intends to expose in chapter XXIII of Book II; Locke's 'I know not what' is unnatured, a bare something. But this makes little difference to our argument, since the general property of extension does not individuate the piece of wax, at least among

other physical things. That property, of course, could tell us that the entity in question is not identical with any mental particular. For an excellent discussion of the problem of what an individual is in Aristotle (and thus, since Descartes has a substance metaphysics, by extension in Descartes) see Ellen Stone Haring's three-part article in *Review of Metaphysics* 10 (1956–7); see especially 316ff. for a discussion of the difficulties of 'prime' matter, that is, bare substrata. The problems of *knowing* the substratum are endemic to the Aristotelian tradition and are, of course, forcefully exposed by both Locke and Berkeley.

19 Thus Descartes has a radical distinction between the semantics for 'a' and the semantics for 'F' in 'Fa.' We see here, we believe, the beginnings of the problems with the unity of perception that exercised Kant. Malebranche has a quite similar problem when he separates sentiments of secondary qualities from those ideas of primary qualities that we see in the mind of God. His solution is to claim that God 'joins' the two in an act of perception. Given the problems about the material world we mentioned in note 12, above, we might speculate that the individuation problem for Malebranche becomes a function of the role of secondary qualities. See *Dialogues*, Dialogue V, especially 111ff.

20 That is, our language (analogous here to our ideas) is consistent, as far as our behaviour towards the world is concerned, with an infinite number of different possible worlds. As Quine argues (in *Word and Object*, 68ff.), there are an infinite number of what came to be called 'translation manuals' consistent with our current language and behaviour; if we think of each such manual as representing a possible world, then our analogy says that an infinite number of possible worlds might produce the ideas we have.

21 Although we shall not argue it here, we believe there is an interesting relationship between the 'generalized inverted spectrum' problem and the more traditional 'Molyneux' problem.

22 Given Descartes's inability to deal successfully with the first demon, it is not difficult to see why Malebranche and Leibniz are so worried about the causal relation, or lack of it, between mind and body. As we have said, the physical world, the brain state, is, in Descartes's words, the occasion for the triggering of some innate mechanisms. This notion of causation is left after the constraints of the *ex nihilo* principle have seemingly been satisfied: we still need to worry about what our ideas reveal about the physical world. It is a short step to occasionalism and pre-established harmony to forge some sort of guarantee that both allows for error in judgment and side-steps the possibility of systematic error. Seen in this way, both occasionalism and pre-established harmony are merely different forms of the same guarantee from God that Descartes invokes in the Sixth Meditation. For the empiri-

cists, however, it is an even shorter step to a full-blown Humean causality which, in its full logical sweep, carries away with it even the *ex nihilo* principle.

23 Tyler Burge, 'Cartesian Error and the Objectivity of Perception.'
24 Ibid., 128–9.
25 Ibid., 129.
26 Ibid., 131.
27 Ibid., 121.
28 The difficulties posed by the first demon should be of little surprise to those used to the problems engendered by the separation of meaning and truth. Russell believed that Frege had parallel difficulties. In Descartes's case, he cannot account for the meaningfulness of ideas without exemplars and a physical world. But in so far as ideas themselves go, no other ontological commitment is necessary.

5: A New Approach to Berkeley's Ideal Reality

An earlier version of this chapter was a co-winner of the Colin and Alisa Turbayne International Berkeley Essay Prize Competition for 1993.

1 For a review of much of the more recent argumentation see George Pappas, 'Ideas, Minds, and Berkeley.'
2 See Phillip D. Cummins, 'Berkeley's Likeness Principle.'
3 Only Chisholm followers, for example, Pitcher, have offered any plausible explanation of Berkeley's move here. G.E. Moore, of course, made much of the collapse in 'The Refutation of Idealism,' but he did not adequately explain Berkeley's motivation for it. Perhaps the general decline in the importance of the act that has marked so much of contemporary philosophy has been reflected in historical scholarship as well.
4 If Dennett is right, an act of awareness of a representation calls for another act of awareness, now of the representation of the representation. One could think of this – we think Dennett does – as a series of homunculi reading a series of representations.
5 We describe the first- and third-person points of view in considerable detail in later chapters. We also discuss Berkeley's misplaced confidence that we experience sensible qualities directly and that this is a matter of common sense.
6 George Berkeley, 'Three Dialogues between Hylas and Philonous,' 167.
7 George Berkeley, 'A Treatise Concerning the Principles of Human Knowledge,' 73.
8 But this move alone does not allow a final characterization of Berkeley's

notion of the mental. Berkeley insists that ideas are passive. This characterization does not change even if ideas are classified as acts. In other words, it
does not help to claim ideas are mental just because they inhere in mental
substances, even if ideas are acts, unless one can give an independent characterization of why such substances are mental by 'nature.' Characterizing
mental substance as the seat of volition will not do. For Berkeley, after all,
takes all perception to be passive.

Our argument combines arguments from the *Principles* and the *Dialogues*
in what we think is the logical order of Berkeley's progression to idealism.
The merger is a necessary consequence of the fact, which many commentators have noted, that arguments for the crucial claim that sensible qualities
are mental are almost entirely lacking in the *Principles*.

9 See Edwin B. Allaire, 'Berkeley's Idealism,' and Richard A. Watson, *The
Breakdown of Cartesian Metaphysics*. Pappas ('Ideas, Minds, and Berkeley')
reviews the difficulties with this account. We also believe we provide a more
consistent interpretation overall than the highly interesting analysis presented by Pappas ('Abstract Ideas and the "esse is percepi" Thesis'), which
attributes Berkeley's idealism to a denial of abstract ideas.

10 We examine the place of 'perceptual relativity' arguments in the seventeenth-
century move to the theory of ideas in chapter 7. For a detailed, new, and
interesting account of the place of Berkeley's relativity arguments in his
move towards idealism see Robert Muehlmann, *Berkeley's Ontology*.

11 Berkeley, *Dialogues*, 174–5.

12 Ibid., 203.

13 Ibid., 206.

14 Ibid., 44.

15 Berkeley is very much aware of the arguments of the new science in this
regard. See, for just one example, Berkeley, *Dialogues*, 186.

16 Watson argues this at length in *The Breakdown of Cartesian Metaphysics*.

17 Descartes, CSM1, 304, 152–4.

18 Two papers with insights on this issue are Calvin Normore's 'Meaning and
Objective Being: Descartes and His Sources' and John Cottingham's
'Descartes on Colour.'

19 For a contrary view see Robert McKim, 'Berkeley on Private Ideas and Public
Objects.' Berkeley does entertain the view that the awareness of some sensible qualities may remind us of others that are associated with them; thus the
visual presentation of the colour and shape of a rose may remind us of its
smell and feel. But this is not the sense of representation that is crucial to our
– or his – argument.

20 Berkeley, *Dialogues*, 194.

21 G.E. Moore makes a similar point in 'The Refutation of Idealism,' when assessing Berkeley's argument. One could also argue, we think, that Malebranche exploits the same set of distinctions when he claims that primary qualities are outside the mind of the perceiver but not physical. If these entities are mental, that sense of 'mental' is not at all clear.

22 Berkeley, *Dialogues*, 197.

23 It is interesting to speculate that Berkeley's argument here may cut even against what are traditionally called 'direct realist views,' such as the one held by Aquinas. For Aquinas, too, needs intermediaries in the sense of sensible species.

24 Ryle made similar points about acts many years later in *The Concept of Mind*.

25 There is a problem here, of course, since Berkeley collapses the distinction between the sensation and its object in the *Dialogues*, yet insists both there and in the *Principles*, for example, in section 49, that ideas are in the mind as they are perceived by it, as if perception or direct awareness were a *relation* between the substance and its idea.

26 For a discussion of Berkeley's wearing of two different hats here, see Alan Hausman, 'Adhering to Inherence: A New Look at the Old Steps in Berkeley's March to Idealism.' Clearly, Chisholm-like interpretations are those which favour the collapse towards the act.

27 Berkeley, *Principles*, 44–5. See also sections 7 (43–4) and 73 (72–3).

28 Ibid., 70.

29 See note 4, above.

6: Hume's Use of Illicit Substances

1 David Hume, *A Treatise of Human Nature*, 207. All references to the *Treatise* are cited as 'T,' followed by the page numbers.

2 Barry Stroud, *Hume*, 120 and 128.

3 Stroud alludes to the importance of this issue when he wonders what property collects perceptions into a mental bundle. See ibid., 138–9.

4 See, for example, T207.

5 There is another possibility here: that a perception can depend upon a mind, that is, be lawfully connected to it, without being 'in' it, in any plausible sense of 'in.' This important alternative is discussed in detail later.

6 We take off from the places in which H.H. Price's classic discussion of these issues in *Hume's Theory of the External World* fails. Our view of phenomenalism comes from Price; Bertrand Russell's *An Inquiry into Meaning and Truth*; Nelson Goodman's *The Structure of Appearance*; and various works by A.J. Ayer, especially *The Foundations of Empirical Knowledge*.

7 Another resolution of the problem rests on an alleged distinction between reason and the imagination. Hume, it is said, is very interested in the *Treatise* in showing that reason constantly clashes with the imagination, thus producing sceptical dilemmas that can be resolved only by letting nature take its course. Then the specific clash described above is merely one aspect of the general clash between the imagination, which posits the possibility of unsensed perceptions, and reason, which tells us that such a possibility is in fact not actualized. Thus Hume is quite aware, in this interpretation, that there is a conflict between his atomism and the theory of ideas, and he plays off of this conflict consciously and constantly. We do not discuss this possibility here.

8 T633ff.

9 Stroud thinks the problem in the Appendix is that Hume thinks that one's 'gaze' is limited to one's own perceptions; for if one's gaze is so limited, there is no problem about getting an idea of the self, as Hume thinks the vulgar idea arises. He believes that if Hume did not assume one's gaze was so restricted, then he couldn't account for our idea of ourselves. He thus thinks that Hume's problem in the Appendix has to do with accounting, not for the self, but for our idea of it as a unified entity. But why does Hume assume that one's gaze is limited one's own perceptions? Does he have Berkeley's early view that to be is to be perceived by *the perceiver*? See Stroud, *Hume* 136ff.

10 This is certainly the view of Russell and the positivists, who made Hume a hero because they felt – unjustifiably, as we shall see – that he was the first genuinely neutral phenomenalist.

11 This connection is explored in Alan Hausman's, 'Adhering to Inherence: A New Look at the Old Steps in Berkeley's March to Idealism.'

12 See especially Nelson Goodman, *The Structure of Appearance*.

13 Thus, though common sense, or a philosopher's version of it, might insist on some sort of 'given,' Goodman insists that it is not necessary to make such an assumption in order to reconstruct the physical and the mental.

14 We question this belief towards the end of this chapter.

15 See Alan Hausman, 'Goodman's Perfect Communities,' 185–8.

16 We have not tried to use other terms that traditionally mark this distinction, for example, public–private, objective–subjective, because we think they have more pejorative implications than our own. We are not, of course, interested in defending the distinction; indeed, in chapter 7 we attack it. Here we are merely calling attention to two long traditions that begin with Descartes. See, for example, C.D. Broad's discussion in chapter 4 of *The Mind and Its Place in Nature*. Another classic discussion is in Arthur O. Lovejoy's *The Revolt against Dualism*, 157ff.

17 For the sake of our argument, we take the laws of science to be free of meta-physical implications. This supposition functions in an important way in our later statement of the argument from perceptual variation.

18 Bertrand Russell, *The Problems of Philosophy*, 7–45.

19 An excellent discussion of the seventeenth-century substance tradition in general, and of mental substance in particular, is in Louis E. Loeb's *From Descartes to Hume*.

20 See note 8, chapter 5.

21 Ideas are effects, so one might try to place the asymmetrical nature of ideas here, in their alleged 'passivity.' But events in the physical world can be effects and not be intentional.

22 In broad terms, this is the view of Aquinas (which we take as typical of the medievals) presented by Etienne Gilson in *History of Christian Philosophy in the Middle Ages*, 377ff. See also Edward P. Mahoney, 'Sense, Intellect, and Imagination in Albert, Thomas, and Siger,' and an excellent discussion of Aquinas's theory of intentionality in Anthony L. Lisska, 'Axioms of Intentionality in Aquinas' Theory of Knowledge.'

23 See our discussion of intentionality in chapter 2.

24 Lisska, 'Axioms of Intentionality in Aquinas' Theory of Knowledge,' 314ff.

25 It would thus be easy to assimilate the problem to the general problem of the interaction between the physical and the mental. Aquinas does not seem to have this latter difficulty.

26 Presumably this would work, at least in Descartes's case, by appeal to the nature of mental substance as a thinking thing. Ideas would be 'structured,' as it were, by this essence, hence intentional; they would represent an unfolding of the nature of the mental.

27 We think this is one plausible way of reading Locke's claims, that ideas represent and that there are no natured mental substances.

28 See Stroud, *Hume*, ch. 2, and especially 26.

29 Ibid., 96ff. The distinction between accounting for the acquisition of the ideas of continuing and independent existence, and accounting for the belief that those ideas apply to anything, is discussed below.

30 As will become clear, the issues we are interested in with respect to justification of our belief in the continuing existence of bodies are raised by Hume independently of worries about justification of *any* induction, whether about continuing bodies or not.

31 Price, *Hume's Theory of the External World*, 6ff., and 53ff. This point is a focus of Price's book. But not all commentators think the point important. Stroud does not even mention the apparent discrepancy between the earlier and later view concerning the place of causation in reasoning to and believing in

the existence of unperceived bodies; indeed, he concentrates on a different aspect of Hume's account of continuing existence – namely, Hume's attempt at explaining the constancy of our perceptions, for example, in the case of seeing a mountain, looking away, then looking back.

32 Stroud, *Hume*, 106.

33 Given that we are not justified in filling gaps in our perceptions by inductive means, Hume cannot give the ordinary phenomenalistic reconstruction of physical objects. It is only when his idealism is ignored that one can construe Hume in the way that many twentieth-century philosophers themselves construe him – as their forefather.

34 As memory is simply a string of ideas accurately reproducing the order of the original entrance of impressions, and belief an idea with sufficient force and vivacity, so all mental acts are nothing more than the occurrence of impressions or ideas. For Hume we cannot say, as Hylas would have wished, that the properties of the act of perceiving, as act, are very different than the properties of the object of that act, as object. On this matter Hume is totally committed: the object of perception and the act of perception are one.

35 See T211.

36 This leaves Hume's reasons for introducing perceptual variation at this point in his analysis in doubt. We take up perceptual variation in detail in chapter 7.

7: Berkeley and the Argument from Perceptual Variation

1 Robert Muehlmann's recent analysis of the argument from perceptual variation (in *Berkeley's Ontology*) arrives at a conclusion with which we agree: the argument alone does not establish idealism. However, Muehlmann seems to believe that the argument is effective in Berkeley's eyes only against the naïve materialist view that all perceivable qualities are qualities of some material thing. We think that the argument does more than this for Berkeley, even if he himself does not explicitly recognize it.

2 Although we shall not argue the case here, our argument against Berkeley equally applies to Hume.

3 Given Descartes's discussions of error in the *Meditations*, it is tempting to take this view. We shall not argue the point here, but we believe that Descartes does not use the problem of perceptual variation to arrive at the theory of ideas. However, even if Descartes did so use perceptual variation, his theory of ideas is radically different from Berkeley's. The theory of ideas of Berkeley is not representational in the sense that Descartes's is, if it is representational at all. This is one of the anomalies of his adoption of the

view that what is perceived directly is mental; he has no appearance–reality distinction in the sense that Descartes does.

4 We shall not give here the extensive set of quotations from the *Dialogues* which constitute what we call Berkeley's argument from perceptual variation (not all the arguments in the first Dialogue fit this mould, of course). Though many of them invoke the perceptual apparatus of other animals, for example, mites, there is a strong clear appeal to the relativity of perception which, as we shall show using Austin and Ayer, is the heart of the matter.

5 We are heavily indebted to Austin's discussion, especially of A.J. Ayer's *The Foundation of Empirical Knowledge*, in what follows. See J.L. Austin, *Sense and Sensibilia*, 28ff., for his discussion of normal adult perceivers. We should add that Ayer attempts to answer Austin's criticisms in 'Has Austin Refuted the Sense-Datum Theory?'

6 A marvellous anticipation of Austin's argument (his ch. 4) is found in Thomas Reid, *Essays on the Intellectual Powers of Man*, Essay II.

7 Just as Austin, in answering the question 'What is the shape of a cat?,' would say that it depends on the context (on what it is doing), so the question 'How does the coin look?' must be answered in the same way (from what perspective you are seeing it). To put it in more traditional terms, the predicate in question is not merely 'appears oval' but 'appears oval-under-conditions-C.' See Austin, *Sense and Sensibilia*, ch. 3.

8 The argument that follows would be the same if F did not know the laws of perspective, and so on, though it is not clear that anyone is ever in such a position. We discuss this possibility along with the first-person perspective later in this chapter.

9 One way to see the difference between Austin and Ayer is to recognize that Austin refuses to distinguish judgments from sensations, or direct awarenesses, as Ayer must do. That is why Austin refuses to allow that, when one sees a pig before one, one is judging on the basis of an induction from sensations that one sees a pig, and thus could be mistaken about it. See Austin, *Sense and Sensiblia*, 48ff.

10 It is one of the ironies of this debate that Ayer agrees that there can be no shapes without something shaped. But rather than deny the existence of the oval shape, he posits the existence of something that does have it, a sense datum. The slide between sensations and sense data is notorious in this dialectic.

11 Is there an independent phenomenalistic viewpoint? Twentieth-century criticism has shown that such a point of view is fraught with difficulty. That one is ever in the position of not knowing any laws is suspect. That there is a vocabulary of predicates that refers to a unique set of phenomenal qualities is today associated with the notion of the given, which so many abjure.

12 Whatever use he makes of them, Descartes's arguments in the first two meditations are surely the most famous and precedent-setting modern examples
of the argument of 'no intrinsic difference.'

13 We find it ironic that Berkeley, especially in the *Dialogues*, uses the argument
from error and illusion to establish a 'no intrinsic difference' argument and
then, because of that argument, moves to F's viewpoint. For, as we have
pointed out, using the 'no intrinsic difference' argument involves abstracting
qualities, and Berkeley argues vehemently against just this sort of abstraction
in both the *Dialogues* and the *Principles*. Berkeley insists that one is never
aware of qualities alone, but always individuated in some way, so that what
one is abstracting is, to say the least, unclear.

14 Bertrand Russell, *The Problems of Philosophy*, ch. 1. We explore Russell's reasoning in more detail later in this chapter.

15 See Nelson Goodman, *The Structure of Appearance*, ch. 4.

16 However, this will not be a different *ontological* category; both sets of data are
among our ideas.

17 Austin seems to believe that the whole theory of ideas stems from the common errors concerning perceptual variation made by both Descartes and the
empiricists. For one of Hume's views, which does seem to fit Russell's argument, see T210–11.

18 Let us be clear that we are not accusing Berkeley of an implicit contradiction
here. As we have maintained above, if the 'no intrinsic difference' argument
works, T's point of view is logically distinct from F's. We wish to maintain,
however, that Berkeley's view that we are directly aware of sensible qualities
makes no sense unless he is *motivated* by the 'perceptual variation' argument.

19 There is another strand in the assumption that one is directly acquainted
with sensible qualities – namely, Berkeley's quite illegitimate assimilation of
the perception of both primary and secondary qualities to the model of feel-
ing pain. Although we shall not press the point here, we believe that Berkeley would never push this rather transparently inept model unless he were
convinced on other grounds that what one is directly aware of are sensations
identified in the sense-data way. As we mentioned earlier, there is a constant
slide, by those using perceptual variation, between sensations and sense
data.

Epilogue

1 Bertrand Russell, *The Problems of Philosophy*, ch. 1.

2 The problems we refer to here are the Fodor–Dennett problems – the semantic and syntactic problems that Descartes tries to solve, as we outlined them

in chapters 2–4, and not necessarily the problems with sense data that arise from consideration of the argument from perceptual variation.

3   As we have claimed previously, Descartes could base a scientific psychology on the causal connections between such intentional entities, thereby giving functionalism its due, without giving up his own very different view of semantics.

4   We are of course not arguing that Berkeley thinks that acts with intrinsically *intentional* properties cause the problem, because he did not see clearly what an intentional property could be. Rather, he objects to acts in a somewhat muddled way. As we have explicated this rejection in chapter 5, it is because he thinks that acts, as ordinarily conceived, must bring in information, which he sees as causing intermediary problems. Berkeley simply does not see that such intermediaries need not lead to scepticism if one takes them in a Cartesian way.

5   Berkeley does indicate in section 49 that there is a direct awareness of sensible qualities. This is not a reinstatement of mental acts, but merely a half-hearted recognition that there must be something different about the mind when one perceives sensible qualities than when one does not.

6   See George S. Pappas, 'Ideas, Minds, and Berkeley.'

7   It is ironic that Moore's point became the inspiration for the Inherence Account, in that Moore talks of the quality blue being taken as a property of the act of awareness of it. In taking over that point and replacing the act of perceiving blue with mental substance (see Alan Hausman's 'Adhering to Inherence: A New Look at the Old Steps in Berkeley's March to Idealism'), the Inherence Account drops from consideration the collapse of act and object. Our reinstatement of the importance of the collapse shows that the Inherence Account is at best only a partial picture of Berkeley's move to idealism.

References

Adams, Robert Merrihew. 'Where Do Our Ideas Come From – Descartes *vs.* Locke.' In *Innate Ideas*, ed. Stephen P. Stich, 71–87. Berkeley: University of California Press, 1975.

Allaire, Edwin B. 'Berkeley's Idealism.' *Essays in Ontology* 1 (1963), 92–105.

Austin, J.L. *Sense and Sensibilia*. New York: Oxford University Press, 1964.

Ayer, Alfred J. *The Foundations of Empirical Knowledge*. London: Macmillan, 1960.

– 'Has Austin Refuted the Sense-Datum Theory?' *Synthese* 17 (1967), 117–40.

Bennett, Jonathan. 'Descartes's Theory of Modality.' *The Philosophical Review* 103 (1994), 639–67.

Bergmann, Gustav. 'Acts.' In *Logic and Reality*, 3–44. Madison: University of Wisconsin Press, 1964.

– 'Intentionality.' In *Meaning and Existence*, 3–38. Madison: University of Wisconsin Press, 1960.

Berkeley, George. *A Treatise Concerning the Principles of Human Knowledge*. In *The Works of George Berkeley, Bishop of Cloyne*, ed. A.A. Luce and T.E. Jessop, vol. 2: 19–113. London: Thomas Nelson and Sons.

– *Three Dialogues between Hylas and Philonous*. In *The Works of George Berkeley, Bishop of Cloyne*, ed. A.A. Luce and T.E. Jessop, vol. 2: 163–263. London: Thomas Nelson and Sons.

Boolos, George S., and Richard C. Jeffrey. *Computability and Logic*, 2d ed. London: Cambridge University Press, 1980.

Broad, C.D. *The Mind and Its Place in Nature*. London: Routledge and Kegan Paul, 1951.

Burge, Tyler. 'Cartesian Error and the Objectivity of Perception.' In *Subject, Thought, and Content*, ed. Philip Pettit and John McDowell, 117–36. Oxford: Clarendon Press, 1986.

Churchland, Paul M. *Matter and Consciousness*. Cambridge, MA: MIT Press, 1984.

Cottingham, John. 'Descartes on Colour.' *Proceedings of the Aristotelian Society* 90 (1989–90), 231–46.

Cummins, Phillip D. 'Berkeley's Likeness Principle.' In *Locke and Berkeley: A Collection of Critical Essays*, ed. C.B. Martin and D.M. Armstrong, 353–63. Notre Dame, IN: University of Notre Dame Press, 1968.

Curley, E.M. 'Descartes on the Creation of the Eternal Truths.' *The Philosophical Review* 93 (1984), 569–97.

Danto, Arthur. 'The Representational Character of Ideas and the Problem of the External World.' In *Descartes: Critical and Interpretive Essays*, ed. Michael Hooker, 287–97. Baltimore, MD: Johns Hopkins University Press, 1978.

Dennett, Daniel C. *Brainstorms*. Cambridge, MA: Bradford Books, 1978.

Descartes, René. *The Philosophical Writings of Descartes*, 2 vols. Trans. John Cottingham, Robert Stoothoff, and Dugald Murdoch. Cambridge: Cambridge University Press, 1988.

Fodor, Jerry A. 'The Mind–Body Problem.' *Scientific American* 244 (Jan. 1981), 114–23.

Frankfurt, Harry. 'Descartes on the Creation of Eternal Truths.' *The Philosophical Review* 88 (1979), 55–91.

Gilson, Etienne. *History of Christian Philosophy in the Middle Ages*. New York: Random House, 1954.

Goodman, Nelson. *Languages of Art*. New York: Bobbs-Merrill, 1968.

– *The Structure of Appearance*. Boston: D. Reidel, 1977.

Haring, Ellen Stone. 'Substantial Form in Aristotle's *Metaphysics Z*.' *Review of Metaphysics* 10 (1956–7), 308–32 (Part I), 482–513 (Part II), 698–713 (Part III).

Hausman, Alan. 'Adhering to Inherence: A New Look at the Old Steps in Berkeley's March to Idealism.' *Canadian Journal of Philosophy* 14/3 (1984), 421–43.

– 'Goodman's Perfect Communities.' *Synthese* 41 (1979), 185–237.

– 'Innate Ideas.' In *Studies in Perception*, ed. Peter K. Machamer and Robert G. Turnbull, 200–30. Columbus: Ohio State University Press, 1978.

– 'Review of Watson's *The Breakdown of Cartesian Metaphysics*.' *Nous* 27/2 (1993), 272–5.

Hintikka, Jaako. '*Cogito Ergo Sum*: Inference or Performance?' *The Philosophical Review* 71 (1962), 3–32.

Hume, David. *A Treatise of Human Nature*, ed. L.A. Selby-Bigge; 2d. ed., rev. by P.H. Nidditch. Oxford: Oxford University Press, 1978.

Jolley, Nicholas. 'Leibniz and Malebranche on Innate Ideas.' *The Philosophical Review* 97 (1988), 71–92.

Kennington, Richard. 'The Finitude of Descates's Evil Genius.' *Journal of the History of Ideas* 32 (1971), 441–6.

Lennon, Thomas A. 'Philosophical Commentary.' In *Nicolas Malebranche*. Trans. Lennon and Paul Olscamp, 757–848. Columbus: Ohio State University Press, 1980.

Lisska, Anthony L. 'Axioms of Intentionality in Aquinas' Theory of Knowledge.' *International Philosophical Quarterly* 16/4 (1976), 305–22.

Loeb, Louis E. *From Descartes to Hume*. Ithaca, NY: Cornell University Press, 1981.

Loux, Michael. *Universals and Particulars: Readings in Ontology*. Notre Dame, IN: University of Notre Dame Press, 1976.

Lovejoy, Arthur O. *The Revolt against Dualism*. La Salle, IL: Open Court, 1960.

Lycan, William G., ed. *Mind and Cognition: A Reader*. Cambridge, MA: Basil Blackwell, 1990.

Mahoney, Edward P. 'Sense, Intellect, and Imagination in Albert, Thomas, and Siger.' In *The Cambridge History of Later Medieval Philosophy*, ed. Norman Kretzmann, 602–22. Cambridge: Cambridge University Press, 1982.

Malebranche, Nicholas. *Dialogues on Metaphysics*. Trans. Willis Doney. New York: Abaris Books, 1980.

– *The Search after Truth*. Trans. and ed. by Thomas M. Lennon and Paul J. Olscamp. Columbus: Ohio State University Press, 1980.

Maull, Nancy. 'Cartesian Objects and the Geometrization of Nature.' In *Descartes: Philosophy, Mathematics and Physics*, ed. Stephen W. Gaukroger, 23–40. Sussex: Harvester, 1980.

McKim, Robert. 'Berkeley on Private Ideas and Public Objects.' In *Minds, Ideas, and Objects: North American Kant Society Studies in Philosophy*, vol. 2, ed. Phillip D. Cummins and Guenter Zoeller, 215–33. Alta Dena, CA: Ridgeview, 1993.

Moore, G.E. 'The Refutation of Idealism.' In *Philosophical Studies*, 1–30. Patterson, NJ: Littlefield, Adams, 1959.

Muehlmann, Robert. *Berkeley's Ontology*. Indianapolis, IN: Hackett, 1992.

Normore, Calvin. 'Meaning and Objective Being: Descartes and His Sources.' In *Essays on Descartes' Meditations*, ed. Amelie Rorty, 223–41. Berkeley: University of California Press, 1986.

Pappas, George S. 'Abstract Ideas and the 'esse is percepi' Thesis.' *Hermanthena* 139 (1985), 47–62.

– 'Ideas, Minds, and Berkeley.' *American Philosophical Quarterly* 17/3 (1980), 181–94.

Pitcher, George. *Berkeley*. London: Routledge and Kegan Paul, 1984.

Price, H.H. *Hume's Theory of the External World*. Oxford: Clarendon Press, 1967.

Quine, Willard Van Orman. *Word and Object*. New York: John Wiley and Sons, 1960.

Reid, Thomas. *Essays on the Intellectual Powers of Man.* Cambridge, MA: MIT Press, 1969.

Russell, Bertrand. *An Inquiry into Meaning and Truth.* Baltimore, MD: Penguin, 1962.

– *Introduction to Mathematical Philosophy.* London: George Allen and Unwin, 1956.

– *The Problems of Philosophy.* London: Oxford University Press, 1968.

Ryle, Gilbert. *The Concept of Mind.* New York: Barnes and Noble, 1961.

Searle, John R. *The Rediscovery of the Mind.* Cambridge, MA: MIT Press, 1992.

Stace, W.T. *A Critical History of Greek Philosophy.* London: Macmillan, 1960.

Stroud, Barry. *Hume.* London: Routledge and Kegan Paul, 1977.

Thomason, Richmond H. *Symbolic Logic.* Toronto: Macmillan, 1970.

Watson, Richard A. *The Breakdown of Cartesian Metaphysics.* Atlantic Highlands, NJ: Humanities Press, 1987.

Weinberg, Julius R. 'Cogito, Ergo, Sum: Some Reflections on Mr. Hintikka's Article.' *The Philosophical Review* 71 (1962), 483–91.

Wilson, Margaret D. *Descartes.* London: Routledge and Kegan Paul, 1978.

Name Index

Subject Index